THE NATIONAL PURPOSE
RECONSIDERED

THE NATIONAL PURPOSE
RECONSIDERED

Dona Baron, Editor

New York   Columbia University Press   1978

Library of Congress Cataloging in Publication Data

Baron, Dona, 1943–
  The national purpose reconsidered.

  Includes bibliographical references and index.
  1. United States—Civilization—1945–
—Addresses, essays, lectures. I. Title.
E169.12.B297   973.92   78-6103
ISBN 0-231-04472-0

Columbia University Press
New York   Guildford, Surrey
Copyright © 1978 Columbia University Press
All rights reserved
Printed in the United States of America

To my Mother and Father

CONTENTS

PREFACE

As THE CENTERPIECE of its program commemorating the National Bicentennial, during the fall of 1976 Columbia University presented a series of symposia entitled "The National Purpose Reconsidered: 1776–1976." The object of this interdisciplinary undertaking was to encourage some of America's, and the world's, most interesting minds to focus upon a reinterpretation of the American experience from the vantage points of their particular experience and expertise. This volume includes five of the six essays prepared for the series as well as a "Historical Prologue" by Richard B. Morris, Gouverneur Morris Professor of History Emeritus and Principal Director of the series, and my concluding chapter, "The National Purpose Reconsidered: A Post-Bicentennial Perspective."

A grant from the National Endowment for the Humanities was the primary source of funding for the series of symposia and the publication of this volume. Additional and significant funding for the symposia came from the Gino Speranza Lecture Fund, which was established in 1952 by a bequest of Mr. Speranza's wife, the late Florence Colgate Speranza, to provide lectures devoted to "American traditions and ideals, viewed from a historical viewpoint."

At each symposium an eminent member of the Columbia community introduced the principal speaker. His lecture was followed by comments provided by two distinguished Columbia faculty members who had advance copies of the address. The insights and counterpoints of the introductions and comments contributed notably to the quality of the series and are reflected in the Preface and in the concluding chapter.

George W. Ball was invited to reflect upon "America's Changing World Posture." His credentials as a specialist in international law and economics as well as his long and distinguished record of public service commended him for this difficult assignment. Under-Secretary of State during the Kennedy and Johnson administrations and, later, U.S. Ambassador to the United Nations, Ball was one of the very few then influential foreign affairs experts to have opposed, from its beginnings, the escalation of U.S. involvement in Vietnam. Ball's *Diplomacy for a Crowded World* was published in 1976. An attorney and investment banker, currently a senior partner of Lehman Brothers, Ball was at the time of his participation in this series an adviser to presidential candidate Jimmy Carter.[1]

Martin E. Marty, who addressed himself to "The Changing Role of Religion in American Society," is superbly qualified to meet the challenge of this topic. A specialist in the history of modern Christianity at the Divinity School of the University of Chicago, Marty is a scholar of interdisciplinary bent, an ordained minister who has tended a parish, and an active journalist. He has served as associate editor of *The Christian Century* since 1963 and has written numerous books and articles, many dealing with questions of religion in America, including: *The New Shape of American Religion* (1959); *The Infidel: Freethought and American Religion* (1961); *Righteous Empire, the Protestant Experience in America* (1970); and *The Pro and Con Book of Religious America* (1975).[2]

The topic "A New Historic Passage: Energy, the Economy, and the Era of Constraints" was appropriately chosen for this series by Dr. Barry Commoner. Introducing Commoner to his Columbia audience, Peter Likins, Dean of the School of Engineering and Applied Science, aptly made the point that while Commoner is best known as an advocate of the cause of ecology and as an active and outspoken critic of public policy as well as of "certain sectors of the American establishment," he also has earned notable credentials in the academic realm of research with his work in cell biology, especially plant viruses. Drawn by his social concerns to fields well beyond the area of his original expertise, Commoner is now University Professor of Environmental Science at Washington University in St. Louis and Director of its Center for the Biology of Natural Systems. Commoner attained prominence in the environmentalist movement with the 1971 publication of *The Closing Circle*, which spelled out for the general reader the ominous impact modern technology could have upon the environment and society. In his 1976 book, *The Poverty of Power*, Commoner explored the energy crisis and the broader economic malaise.[3]

More than three decades after publication of *An American Dilemma*, Dr. Gunnar Myrdal was invited to reexamine with the perspective of time some of the central concerns of that classic study. Thus Myrdal, termed by Herbert Gans, Professor of Sociology and Senior Research Associate, Center for Policy Research, who commented on his lecture,[4] "the best foreign analyst of American society since Tocqueville," provides us with his most recent observations on "Race and Class in a Welfare State." Recipient of the 1974 Nobel Prize for Economics, Professor of International Economics at the Institute for International Economic Studies in Stockholm, Myrdal is a prolific author whose books include: *Monetary Equilibrium* (1939); *Rich Lands and Poor* (1958); *Beyond the Welfare State* (1960); and *The Asian Drama* (1968). He has been a dedicated leader and public servant both in his native Sweden, where he has served in various capacities, including Minister of Commerce, and for international organizations, notably as Secretary General of the U.N. Economic Commission for Europe during the crucial years, 1947–57. Myrdal also has special ties with America. Aside from his exploration of American racial relations in *An American Dilemma*, Myrdal has constantly renewed his contacts with the United States. Most recently he served during 1974–75 as Morton Globus Visiting Distinguished Professor of Social Science at the City College of the City University of New York.

John Doar, who treated the theme "Civil Rights and Self-Government," fittingly chose to focus upon the major constitutional crises with which he was intimately associated: the civil rights revolution and Watergate. Doar has compiled a record of public service marked distinctively by integrity and achievement. Named Deputy Assistant Attorney General of the Civil Rights Division of the Department of Justice during the Eisenhower administration, Doar continued in that capacity through the Kennedy administration, becoming head of the division under President Lyndon B. Johnson. He prosecuted voting rights cases and rode with Freedom Riders. Both the significance of Doar's achievements as a participant in these moving events as well as his courage were underscored by Professor of Law Louis Lusky,[5] who, in his comments upon the lecture, recalled this telling episode: After the murder of Medgar W. Evers, in Jackson, Mississippi, a mob of furious blacks armed with bottles and rocks found themselves confronted by a double line of policemen, ready to use their clubs and guns. Alone, John Doar moved into the space between the two groups, announced, "My name is John Doar and anybody around here knows I stand for what is right," and proceeded to plead—successfully—for restraint. Doar later served as President of the New York City Board of Education, and as Director of the Bedford-Stuyvesant Development and Services Corporation in Brooklyn. As Chief Counsel for the impeachment investigation of the House Committee on the Judiciary, Doar displayed his ability to gather and marshal facts dispassionately as well as his deeply felt commitment to the constitutional system. He is currently an attorney with Donovan, Leisure, Newton, and Irvine in New York City.

The lecture by Dr. Donald S. Frederickson, Director of the National Institutes of Health, entitled "The Public Governance of Science," will be published in *Man and Medicine; the Journal of Values and Ethics in Health Care*, probably a more appropriate vehicle for consideration of such questions of contemporary significance as the proper extent of government regulation of biomedical research.[6]

In order to present these essays in an appropriate historical context, Richard B. Morris has written a "Historical Prologue." Morris' writings have encompassed an encyclopedic range, including pioneer work in American legal and labor history, and the diplomacy of the American Revolution. Among his books are: *The Peacemakers* (1965); *The American Revolution Reconsidered* (1967); *Seven Who Shaped Our Destiny* (1973); and *John Jay: The Making of a Revolutionary* (1975). In recognition of his distinction, especially as a historian of the colonial and revolutionary periods, his colleagues elected him President of the American Historical Association during the Bicentennial Year.

My concluding chapter seeks to set the contributions to the series in the context of our times and reflects upon the enduring values of the American national purpose amidst the challenges of the recent past and the trials that lie ahead.

The efforts of a good many people at Columbia University contributed to making the series of symposia a reality. Among them were William J. McGill, the President of the university, who strongly supported this project as most suitable for a historic university's commemoration of the Bicentennial, and Wm. Theodore deBary, Executive Vice-President for Academic Affairs and Provost, whose office was responsible for the administrative direction of the project. Doctors McGill and deBary each introduced the major speaker of a symposium, as did other high officials of Columbia: James S. Young, Vice-President for Academic Planning and Professor of Government; Paul Marks, Vice-President for Health Sciences, Frode Jensen, Professor of Medicine and Professor of Human Genetics and Development; Mitchell Ginsberg, Dean of the School of Social Work; and Peter Likins, Dean of the School of Engineering and Applied Science.

Without the indefatigable efforts of Richard B. Morris neither the symposia series nor a number of other university-wide projects commemorating the Bicentennial would have taken place. Claudia Glassman was the vital nexus who day by day made the symposia happen. Special acknowledgement ought to be given as well to James P. Lewis, Director, Office of Projects and Grants; Ene Servet, Associate Editor of the Papers of John Jay; J. Michael Luttig of Washington, D.C.; Elaine Brown, now at Brooklyn Law School, and Robert F. Moss of New York City. Finally, my husband, Jeffrey B. Morris, merits special thanks. Though charged last year with demanding responsibilities as Judicial Fellow at the United States Supreme Court, he gave unstintingly of his time—to advise, to offer editorial suggestions and, perhaps most important, to sustain morale.

D.B.
February 1978

Notes

[1] Commentators for Ball's lecture were Richard D. Gardner, then Henry L. Moses Professor of Law and International Organization, now U.S. Ambassador to Italy; and Marshall D. Shulman, then Adlai E. Stevenson Professor of International Relations and Director of the Russian Institute and now Special Consultant to the Secretary of State on Soviet Affairs.

[2] Commentators for the Marty lecture were Donald Shriver, President, Union Theological Seminary and Seymour Seigel, Professor of Ethics, Jewish Theological Seminary.

[3] Commentators for the Commoner lecture were James Rainwater, Professor of Physics and winner of the Nobel Prize in Physics in 1975 and Seymour Melman, Professor of Industrial Engineering.

[4] The other commentator for the Myrdal lecture was Charles V. Hamilton, Wallace S. Sayre Professor of Government.

[5] The other commentator for the Doar lecture was Louis Henkin, Hamilton Fish Professor of International Law and Diplomacy.

[6] Dr. Frederickson was chosen by the faculty of the College of Physicians and Surgeons to participate in this series of symposia because he stands at the interface of government and medicine. Commentators on Dr. Frederickson's address were Dr. Saul Spiegelman, University Professor, Professor of Human Genetics and Development, and Director, Institute of Cancer Research; and Dr. Robert J. Weiss, Professor of Psychiatry and Social Medicine and Director, Center for Community Health Systems.

THE NATIONAL PURPOSE
RECONSIDERED

RICHARD B. MORRIS

1.

HISTORICAL PROLOGUE

EACH ONE of the distinguished contributors to this Columbia Bicentennial Symposium on "The National Purpose Reconsidered" has addressed himself to certain specific issues and concerns of our nation today. The frame of reference for their respective analyses is a set of values and purposes to which the American people have been traditionally committed, values and purposes articulated in the founding years of nationhood and constitution–making. Aside from the pertinence of their remarks to our present condition, their observations serve as a needed reminder of the vast difference between today's social and political order and that prevailing when the nation first emerged, while underscoring at the same time how surprisingly durable many of the traditional values have proven, how they have bridged the vast gap between the generations.

In examining goals and measuring achievements, the symposium's contributors have implicitly used the traditional American value system as a benchmark. It is therefore appropriate that, before accompanying the contributors in their explorations of the contemporary scene, we take a retrospective look at the nation's guiding purposes as they were construed by the Founding Fathers.

1

It is to this latter need that these introductory remarks are addressed.

The nation's original purpose were forged on the anvil of revolution, a revolution that once embarked upon, albeit reluctantly, demanded of the leadership that their cause be justified "to a candid world" in a statement of grievances and a declaration of first principles. Jefferson's eloquent formulation of basic princilples of govermental authority, while familiar in theory to the world of the European Enlightenment, were now, for the first time in history, put into operation. On a new continent, in a new society, these principles assumed a distinctive cast.

Fundamental to the character of the American Revolution was the notion that the people were sovereign and that a republican system of government based upon the consent of the people was innately superior to any other prevailing system. As the Founding Fathers envisioned it, their republic would prove more virtuous than systems embracing hereditary or caste principles of authority. It would command greater moral discipline. It would be more immediately concerned with the welfare of society, and, since the people were sovereign, it would more surely command their allegiance than other systems. Such a republic, they felt, was tailor-made for America, with its exceptional advantages, its boundless resources, and its immense distance from the Old World. Granted that a republican order had a better chance to put down roots in America, the Founding Fathers confidently expected that its successs would serve as a model for all mankind. Thus, a sense of mission was from the start embedded in the national purpose.

That republican system, rooted in notions of popular sovereignty, representative government, and the equality of states, having been created by an act of secession from an empire, was, from the start, avowedly anticolonial. Although anticolonialism was implicit in the American sense of mission, it did not compel intervention by the United States in other people's wars of liberation. The main goal of the early republic was security and survival as an independent republic. To secure that goal, Americans, confronted with prospects of foreign intervention and evidence of secessionist plottings, reformed their governmental structure and adopted a federal Constitution which underpinned the diplomatic and military arms of the state with fiscal powers that could translate empty posturing into some semblance of reality.

To the Founding Fathers, so soon emerged from a lengthy war for independence, survival meant the avoidance of foreign wars and permanent entanglements with the great European powers. For years the notion of a separate destiny was a ruling concept of our foreign policy. America, the early statesmen contended, could best serve the cause of freedom by example while avoiding active intervention in foreign revolutionary movements. Thus, the first President, by his notable Proclamation of Neutrality, sought to keep the nation clear of the European wars that came in the wake of the French Revolution. The United States avoided overt intervention in the Latin American wars for independence and in the Greek and Hungarian revolutions, but no one was left in doubt for a moment about where American sympathies lay. As Secretary of State, John Quincy Adams denounced the notion of intervention in foreign wars, even "wars for freedom," as changing the very foundations of the American government "From *liberty* to *power*." His was still the American position as late as 1851, when President Millard Fillmore declared that the American mission was not to "impose upon other countries our form of government by artifice or force, but to teach by example and show by our success." Perhaps Fillmore's words should be engraved on the portals of a reconstituted CIA.

Indubitably, in the last hundred years the United States has departed widely from the constricting principles of earlier days. Ourselves acquirers of a far-flung empire, we have often failed to implement the rhetoric of such stalwart opponents of colonialism as Woodrow Wilson and Franklin Delano Roosevelt. Too often have Latin American states been viewed as regimes to be manipulated to suit North American interests. The United States, in effect, repudiated Franklin D. Roosevelt's views on the evils of colonialism when it assumed France's burden in Indochina and became bogged down for years in a wasteful and tragic struggle on behalf of an ally lacking both national purpose and a will to fight. Until recently, we manifested more conern about the freedom of peoples

behind the Iron Curtain than about colonial peoples denied their
political freedom by nations with whom we were allied. In alleged
defense of the national interest, we have bolstered dictatorial regimes and seemingly transcended compelling necessities in the extent of such support and in the number of dictators we have embraced.

Such departures from the original national purpose as conceived by the Founding Fathers were not taken without arousing
intense criticism at home from those who pointedly evoked an
earlier countervailing tradition. And while the issues of national
security remain compelling considerations, it is heartening to be
able to point to countervailing trends as examples of the implementation of a basic anticolonial impulse among Americans—the
fulfillment of the pledge to grant the Philippines its independence,
the investing of Puerto Rico with commonwealth status, the admission to full and equal statehood of Alaska and Hawaii, the first
states whose population numbered a majority of inhabitants of
Asian origin, the reconsidering of our status in Panama, and the
attempts to reconcile the concerns of the self-government with
those of national defense in the administering the Trust Territory
of the Pacific Islands.

Admittedly, the global problems of our own day to which
George Ball addresses himself in this volume are of an entirely
different order both of content and magnitude from those which
only distantly impinged on the nascent United States at the end of
the eighteenth century. Then Americans were buoyed by their nation's seeming self-sufficiency in resources, by its prospective har-
vesting of a vast untapped continent. Today our sense of exceptionalism has faded. We are a people of plenty only in a relative
sense, for we are not only dependent upon other nations for critical
resources, but aware of the necessity of sharing our limited resources with the have-not nations. Then we counted upon a vast
ocean to protect us from the embroilments of Europe. Today the
possibility of nuclear warfare has eliminated all sanctuaries.

From our current disenchantment with involvement in distant
foreign wars one is hardly justified in drawing the conclusion that
America has abandoned its concept of mission and no longer has a

special role to play. Contrariwise, as Mr. Ball persuasively argues, the United States, given the present world predicament, should not consider abdicating its leadership initiatives, permitting them to pass to antidemocratic and totalitarian forces. Thus, so soon after America's withdrawal from Southeast Asia, proponents of a renewed United States activism in world affairs have called upon Americans to reexamine our national purpose insofar as it relates to national security and our posture toward the rest of the world.

If America has a commitment to freedom, the decades since World War II have made it painfully clear that there are limits to power, as John Quincy Adams realized a century and a half ago. For America to commit itself to defend freedom anywhere in the world would constitute an imprudent, even bankrupt, proposition, as empty and as misleading as the "captive peoples" resolution of John Foster Dulles. America has indeed great power, but such power should be aware of its limits and responsible in its deployment.

Nowhere has the national purpose been stated more eloquently than in the Preamble to the Constitution. Last but not least of those explicit purposes was that of securing "the Blessings of Liberty to ourselves and our Posterity." How to make liberty secure in their own day and for their children's children was a major preoccupation of the Founding Fathers. Recognizing popular apprehension about the aggrandizement of power, they promulgated novel constitutional principles governing the relation of the state to the people, recognized certain rights of the individual to be inherent, and under the rubric of federalism imposed limitations on the authority of the federal government.

Central to the national purpose was the protection of individual liberty and, save for temporary aberrations like the Alien and Sedition Laws, the early republic operated under great self-discipline. Break-ins à la Watergate, assassination plots, wiretapping, electronic surveillance, the opening of the mails, and the resort to agents provocateurs would have horrified men of Jefferson's generation, men of moral conviction, devoted to the right of privacy and the protection of civil liberties.

In a noble paragraph Jefferson joined the notion of unalienable rights to that of equality. Indeed, that pervasive egalitarianism which foreign observers invariably commented upon seemed to be a distinctive mark of American society. Here feudal and caste distinctions failed to take hold, the spirit of deference was in decline, and manifestations of upward mobility were ubiquitous. True, women were excluded from the political process and their legal rights were circumscribed. So, too, where white bondsmen because they lacked that proof of independence normally regarded as a requisite to political activity. Uncurbed expansionist urgings on the part of American settlers protracted the long conflict between Indian and white man and dictated their view that the Indian must remain outside the constituency.

Most tenacious was the racist thinking that excluded blacks from that equality to which the Declaration of Independence had theoretically committed all Americans. It was this denial that divided the sections as early as the Constitutional Convention. It was this denial that underlay the years of crisis which culminated in civil war. It is this denial whose reparation has been a major theme of American history since Reconstruction.

Fittingly, John Doar and Gunnar Myrdal address themselves to aspects of this problem, the former to the successful implementation of political rights for blacks, rights long denied in clear contravention of the Civil War Amendments. In ending such political discrimination, in breaking down the traditional barriers to voting by blacks, Mr. Doar himself had played a unique and memorable role. Since 1944, when Gunnar Myrdal published his now classical commentary, *An American Dilemma*, an enormous breakthrough has occurred in race relations in America, and it is to that transformation that Mr. Myrdal pays generous tribute. If the stain of racial discrimination may one day be erased from the image of America, if a system of equality both in law and fact may some day coexist for whites, blacks, Mexican Americans, and other groups against whom discrimination has been practiced—not least of all women— it will be because the national purpose has been redefined to fit the morality of our own age, a morality that demands the full implementation of the promise embodied in the Declaration of Independence.

To reshape the national purpose to fit the needs of a society no longer confident of boundless territorial frontiers for settlement and exploitation, of vast untapped resources to be extravagantly pillaged as in the past, must be a major concern of statesmen in our own time. How to protect a fragile environment from the onrushing forces of the nuclear space age technology and a world population explosion pose problems demanding great social discipline and a rethinking of national, not to say, world priorities, problems to which Barry Commoner addresses himself in this book. That a resolution of these problems is a condition of survival, if not for ourselves, certainly for coming generations, and that it cannot be achieved without a new reconciliation of the goals of private enterprise with that of the public welfare must be clear to all reasonable observers.

Lastly, the point might be made that in any reshaping of our national purpose, the fact must be conceded that a moral imperative has continually motivated America and its people. It has motivated American benevolence and it has distinguished America's foreign policy. In no country in the world has organized philanthropy played so pervasive a role as in the United States. No other country has ever mounted a program of aid to foreign lands comparable in its comprehensiveness. some of this munificent bounty may well have been prompted by a sense of urgency about containing communism—notably the Marshall Plan and the Truman Doctrine—and some of it has come with strings attached that seriously qualified a posture of completely disinterested benevolence, but the deeply moral commitment of helping others has tapped a vast reservoir of American idealism and good will, of generosity, and, above all, compassion.

What then, may we ask, is the relevance to our own times of that earlier national purpose which the opening sentence of the federal Constitution so comprehensively defines and upon which the writings of the Founding Fathers serve as a gloss? Clearly the "more perfect Union," first among the purposes for which the new government was formed, embraced a federal structure which has fallen into sad disrepair. As demands for government services mount to an extent never envisaged by any of the early statesmen, even Hamilton, fiscal stringencies plague the operation of state and local governments, and have dictated a massive redistribution of tax revenue, to which the present revenue–sharing program makes only a limited, if essential, contribution.

The establishment of justice is still a central aim of federal and state governments, but ever mounting pressures of civil litigation and the omnipresent threats of augmented crime, both organized and mindless, have taxed the justice system perhaps beyond its present capacity and at times even challenged the power of the government to "insure domestic tranquillity." A look at the national budget suggests that "the common defence" has become a central preoccupation of the federal government, while the promotion of "the general Welfare" now embraces commitments to reduce unemployment, curb inflation, end discrimination, and expand social services and pensions, commitments which would have seemed staggering to the Founding Fathers, envisaging as they did a government of limited powers called upon to perform very limited tasks.

The obligation to secure "the Blessings of Liberty to ourselves and our Posterity" imposes upon the citizenry a constant vigilance, for too often have they observed how the government apparatus has been prepared to subvert personal liberty on grounds of national security. Vigilant as we must remain about liberty at home, we are manifesting increasing concern about the protection of human rights abroad. Critics who view such efforts as making evangelical didacticism a foundation for foreign policy contend that such reiteration might prove counterproductive. Nonetheless such concerns are consistent with older prevailing American notions of mission and constitute a reassertion of long–cherished first principles. These new initiatives in the area of human rights serve to bolster that image of America as an asylum of liberty, a reminder to the world that to the millions of uprooted and displaced persons of our generation the United States is still "the last best hope of man."

Indeed, in the post-Vietnam years much has been accomplished to refurbish the image of America not only as a champion of human rights but as an anticolonial democratic nation. To give substance to the image, America may well be expected to exhibit a greater degree of realism about political systems adopted in less-developed nations, political systems which are neither popular nor democratic in the sense we use the term, and a greater awareness of the role of nationalism, even ultranationalism, in the shaping of countervailing ideologies.

In sum, the creative years of revolution and constitution-making, two hundred years behind us, provide the occasion to reexamine our national purpose and priorities then so eloquently articulated, to redefine and reshape them to fit the national interest as we perceive it in a changing world, and to ensure that generations yet unborn may still enjoy the blessings of liberty under a government freely resting upon the consent of the governed.

GEORGE W. BALL

2.

AMERICA'S CHANGING WORLD POSTURE

MEN AND WOMEN feel an irresistible urge to commemorate mile-stones in the passage of time with rhetorical exercises that attempt to assess where we are, how we got there, and in what direction, if any, we should be going. During this Bicentiennial Year attempts at a national reassessment will fill many large volumes. If they do not point America with certitude in the best possible direction, they may at least create renewed respect for the vision of those remarkable men and women who founded our country, and thus stimulate a revival of pride in what this country stood for, as well as what it has since accomplished. If so, that is justification enough, for we seriously need a counter to the self-deprecation and self-flagellation that have characterized what might be called our post-Vietnam neurosis.

What we should remind ourselves during this Bicentennial is that we Americans have a unique history. From the beginning, our forebears were aware of what some sociologists now call their own "Exceptionalism." As Carl Becker pointed out many years ago, we borrowed heavily from the Judaic idea of a chosen people. We were the "city on . . . a hill," what both Hegel and Tocqueville referred to as "the land of the future." Nor was this optimistic appraisal without substance. Apart from any pretensions to moral superiority, the facts surrounding the creation of the United States set it apart as different from other nations. North America was the last richly endowed land mass with a temperate climate to be populated. As the inheritors of eighteenth-century liberalism, the founders of our nation had a chance to try out on a fresh terrain many of the yeasty ideas of the Age of Reason, unencumbered by ancient rivalries, entrenched positions, and the ossified conventional wisdom of the past. They found a continent to exploit with vast space to provide a new concept of scale and scope. Then, in the nineteenth and twentieth centuries, our national mix was enriched by a massive influx of men and women from central and eastern Europe, disenchanted with the Old World but highly endowed with both ability and ambition.

I shall avoid the stylized academic arguments as to the significance of the frontier, or the impact on our national character of physical, social, and economic mobility, or the virtues of the melting pot as opposed to the values of ethnic diversity. I will address myself not so much to the meaning of America for Americans as to the role of leadership conferred upon us by our history and objective situation.

I recognize that this formulation of the question is likely to evoke challenge, for, as a holdover from the disillusion and revisionist excesses of the Vietnam years, it is still fashionable in some circles to deny that America has any special role and to contend that for Americans to aspire to play the part of leader on the global stage betrays a presumption our record does not justify. Yet, though humility is a virtue we should not disdain, neither can we overlook the reality of the world predicament. If America should fail to assume leadership, that does not mean that other large nations would also abjure such a role, but, rather, that leadership would pass primarily to governments with repressive inclinations and aggressive ambitions.

However much we would like to believe that the Cold War is

ended, no one in his right mind can overlook the fact that the Soviet Union is the only other industrialized country organized on a continent-wide basis, that it commands a huge industrial economy, and that it espouses a system antipathetic to ours. If the United States were to cease playing a world role, there is not the slightest doubt that the Kremlin would exploit the opportunities thus created—and with a considerable chance of success.

Until the end of World War II, Britain and France could exercise a major influence on world affairs through their command of sprawling colonial empires. But now they are stripped back to medium-sized metropolitan dimensions and, until the nations of Western Europe transmute their economic collaboration into effective political unity, they will have neither the resources nor the will to do more than play supporting roles in areas outside the small house of Europe. Nor is the situation any different on the other side of the globe. Japan, denuded of the territories it dominated through conquest, is today a world power only in the economic and financial sectors.

Yet there is no point in punching a straw man. Although, particularly in some academic circles, we may hear grumbling that the assertion of leadership on our part would be presumptuous, that is, at best, a fatuous affectation. Because there is no realistic alternative, the relevant question can no longer be whether we should lead but rather how—and under what circumstances—we should seek to exercise our leadership; for there is little doubt that we have, in recent years, sometimes used our power and influence uncritically.

Nor have we lately done well in the formulation of an agreed national objective. Within the past few years, American policy has concentrated almost exclusively on assuring, in the words of Secretary Kissinger, our "national survival." But that is a question-begging phrase. The survival of the nation as a political entity is neither sufficiently spacious nor precise to satisfy most Americans. What we wish is the survival of the United States not merely as a rich and powerful country but with our values intact and, if possible, enriched. After all, America was dedicated from the outset to protecting the rights of its citizens to life, liberty, and the pursuit of happiness, to use the language of the Declaration of Independence, as well as to hold and dispose of property. Those are the basic rights which, as George Kennan pointed out two decades ago, justified the creation of the United States as a "political society separated from that of other nations."

Thus, it would seem axiomatic that America should, so far as possible, shape its policies to encourage governments that protect individual freedoms and abjure repressive practices, although how far we should go in favoring governments solely because they are committed to the private ownership of property is a more debatable question.

That does not mean, of course, that we should go about seeking to create governments in our own image, since our own system is not universally adaptable. Lately, it has been fashionable in intellectual circles to point out how few governments adhere to democratic practices. Although the breakdown of the great colonial systems led many new nations to adopt constitutions that echoed our own, most of those brave documents have long since been jettisoned or disregarded, as politicans untrained in the democratic tradition have tried to cope with the hard realities of power in new nations beset by staggering economic and social problems. This has even led Daniel P. Moynihan to assert: "Neither liberty nor democracy would seem to be prospering . . . Liberal democracy on the American model increasingly tends to the condition of monarchy in the nineteenth century—a holdover form of government . . . It is where the world was, not where it is going . . . "

Although these words can be largely discounted as Celtic hyperbole, authentic democracy clearly requires the existence of basic conditions that do not now exist in many countries. If democracy is to be more than a facade, there must be a minimal level of literacy and the bulk of the population must live within the nation's economy and not outside it. To be sure, a huge, poor country such as India could until recently maintain democratic forms—proudly boasting that it was the largest democracy in the world—but only a tiny handful of elite actually touched, or were materially touched by, the political process. The very fact that India could switch to an authoritarian system almost overnight without widespread perturbations throughout the country demonstrated that point.

Still, America must put itself on the side of freedom if it is to maintain its national integrity and its authority in the world. We could not long exist as a nation of free peoples if we were condemned to live in a world ocean of despotism with no sense of communion with other free societies. Not only would we suffer from acute loneliness, but we would develop a corrosive kind of siege psychology. Mankind is infinitely suggestible and, sooner or later, we would see our own firm attachment to liberty begin to wither away.

Even in purely tactical terms, the mere manipulation of power to preserve our own national survival is not good enough for the United States. Although realpolitik may have adequately served nineteenth century dynastic rulers not accountable to their people, it is not suited to a democracy that can govern only with the consent of the governed; for Americans are not prepared to make sacrifices over a protracted period to support a policy that has no clearly discernible objective other than the manipulation of power. They must perceive a purpose consistent with national ideals and aspirations.

Nor would it be possible for the United States to sustain the leadership of its alliances with other democratic states unless those states could plainly perceive in American policy elements transcending the pure manipulation of power. Otherwise, they would not trust us, for they remember too well the reversal of alliances that was a customary feature of European balance-of-power politics throughout the nineteenth century. Thus, if United States policy were narrowly focused on national survival and nothing more, it would reinforce the already existing uneasiness that America might be tempted in its bilateral dealings with the Soviet Union to create a "condominium" in which the interests of our European allies would only be counters in a superpower bargain.

Finally, America's influence with the Third World depends to a higher degree than most of us are prepared to admit on our ability to maintain the confidence of the poorer peoples of the world that we are true to our own traditions—a confidence gravely weakened by the excesses of Vietnam and the disclosures of CIA activities. After all, Thomas Jefferson and Tom Paine played a larger part in the disintegration of colonial empires than Marx or Lenin, and the shot heard round the world still has its echoes in Third World capitals, particularly since many leaders in the new countries have been exposed to American education.

But it is far easier to say that America should shape its foreign policy to advance and preserve the cause of individual freedom than it is to carry out that objective within the constraints under which our policy must be conducted. Those constraints are imposed not only by the objective facts of the world situation but by the inadequacies of our past diplomacy, the susceptibilities of the American government to domestic political pressures and the conditioned reflexes of our statesmen.

By far the most hobbling constraint on American policy is still the continued rivalry between the Soviet Union and the United States. In spite of windy talk about a polycentric or a multipolar world—the selection of the term depending on whether one favors Greek or Latin neologisms—the competition of the two dominant centers of power is a controlling political fact. Not only does it severely restrict our freedom of action in dealing with other nations, it threatens our survival as well.

Anyone seriously examining the problem of conducting an effective American policy is necessarily struck by how little détente has altered the basic realities of the East-West struggle, since, in practice, it has been narrowly limited to the conduct of bilateral relations between the Soviet Union and the United States and has not even affected all our bilateral relations. It has not been extended to apply either to the relations of the superpowers with third governments involved in local quarrels or to superpower cooperation in the solution of the great world problems of the future—the excessive rate of population growth, food shortages, raw material stringencies, pollution, and so on.

Yet those two sets of problems manifestly pose a far greater threat of world conflict and world catastrophe than do any breakdown in the direct relations between ourselves and Moscow. Direct relations have long been governed by a built-in constraint in the form of the balance of terror—the nuclear standoff—and so long as the United states maintains nuclear parity and a significant sec-ond-strike capability the possibility that the two nations will delib-erately go to war can presumably be ruled out.

A much more serious danger lies in great power involvement in local quarrels in strategic areas of the world, where the super-powers may be drawn almost imperceptibly into a creeping escala-tion, progressively committing more and more of their power and prestige until they reach the point where a sudden reversal of the fortunes of one or the other of their clients may face them with the alternative of major defeat or direct intervention. Anyone who has read Barbara Tuchman's brilliantly perceptive account of the way in which the great powers of Europe were dragged into war almost against their will in 1914 by their commitment to opposing client states in the Balkans should understand the nature of the process. After all, we Americans did not deliberately attack China in 1950; it was the fact that we and the Chinese were on opposite sides of the Korean War that led to that conflict.

In the much advertised "Statement of Principles Governing the Relations Between the United States and the Soviet Union," which President Nixon and Dr. Kissinger negotiated with the So-viet representatives in May 1972, only a tangential reference was made to third party conflicts. The Soviet Union has, almost by conditioned reflex, supported the opposing side from us not only in Vietnam but in such troubled areas as Angola and the Middle East. In fact, the whole world outside of each superpower's immediate sphere of influence still constitutes a potential battlefield in which Moscow and Washington may wage proxy wars.

The persistence of this East-West rivalry seriously constrains our country in seeking to advance individual freedom through its foreign policy because it makes it possible for governments, pressed to adopt more liberal policies, to threaten to turn to the Soviet Union or Peking as an alternative source of help. Moreover, although it should be apparent that many Third World nations will never improve the lot of their people—or even enjoy adequate economic growth—without major changes in their social and eco-nomic structures, our government is constantly discouraged from

pressing for such changes by fear that the disruption accompanying readjustments may lead to the emergence of governments
friendly to Moscow. It is evident, for example, that the social and
economic structure of most of the nations of Latin America must
be materially altered if American aid is to do more than make the
rich richer. Yet throughout the area we continue to support military regimes in the name of stability, and we are likely to continue
to do so in the future.

I make these quite obvious points to underline the type of
dilemma constantly confronted in the execution of our foreign policy. It is easy to say that the United States should always favor
democratic governments and discriminate against those that adopt
repressive measures, but the issues are far more complex than that.
Each choice must be made in a particular political context and
many elements must be factored into the equation of policy. It
does no good to help democratic governments that are too incom-
petent to rule effectively; for we may only hasten political collapse
and the advent of repression from the left or right. Yet it seems
clear that, during the last few years, we have in many instances
gone too far in the other direction—with the Greek colonels, for
example—in giving our tacit stamp of approval to governments not
only tyrannical but cruel and corrupt. We have tried to buy stability—or rights for our forward bases or intelligence facilities—and
have succeeded only in alienating our friends.

These problems are all too often discussed on the assumption
that governments will respond to American pressures or proposals
rationally and in accord with the best interests of their nations and
of their peoples. But that, of course, is a fiction. Governments must
accommodate to the prevailing political environment, and the
prime concern of every government is to stay in power. So it
should not be surprising that leaders often find it more convenient
to react to American pressures—whether to reform their internal
affairs or to pay for expropriated American property—by dema-
gogic speeches denouncing the United States even at the risk of
losing further American assistance. We must recognize, therefore,
that we can rarely produce the desired result by conditioning our
aid on the adoption of programs of land reform or family planning

or the restructuring of agricultural systems, particularly so long as governments can, as many do, threaten to turn to the Soviet Union if the United States presses them too hard, even though the measures we are proposing are essential for the welfare and development of their own people.

In examining the constraints that inhibit the United States in dealing with other nations, there is one final problem that arises when we seek to help small nations under serious external threat. If we extend assistance to nations on the assumption that our own interests are involved in their security, then, by indulging the freedom to be irresponsible under cover of our protection, the governments of such nations can exploit the leverage of their own weakness. This problem was most vividly exemplified by President Thieu when his government threatened to collapse every time Washington suggested that he strengthen its roots with the people by broadening the political base. He found such threats an effective stratagem; since, faced with the prospects of political uncertainty that might accompany another change of government, we repeatedly gave in to his authoritarian tendencies.

It is a frustrating aspect of the present world situation that whenever we identify the security of other countries with our own security interests, we cannot use the coercive potential of a threat to withdraw our military aid or protection without weakening our own position. That is a lesson it has been hard to learn, yet we see examples of it constantly—in South Korea or in Italy today if we use the prospect of expulsion from NATO as a deterrent to Communist participation in the government.

If the withdrawal of military aid would be self-defeating, economic sanctions may have quite unpredictable consequences. When we employ such sanctions to try to bring about a liberalization of conditions in a foreign country, for example, will we create pressures within the affected country encouraging the government to make the changes demanded, or will we create a siege psychology that operates to consolidate support behind the most obscurantist elements? Although academicans have studied almost every other aspect of foreign policy beyond the point of of diminishing returns, they have paid little scholarly attention to that question. In shaping our policy, we tend to follow the course most congenial to our domestic politics with little attention to obvious contradictions. Thus many Americans who fervently insist that expanding our trade with the Soviet Union will, by opening the doors and windows of a closed society, bring about benign change in its social policies and relations with other countries contend with equal fervor that we should restrict trade and hermetically seal off Rhodesia and South Africa from the outside world in order to promote benign change. Such a paradox might well suggest to the cynical that many favor economic sanctions against unpopular governments with unattractive social policies more because it gives them a glow of righteous satisfaction than from any conviction that it will, in fact, lead to the amelioration of intolerable conditions.

Ambivalence is also apparent in the way we apply the classical injunction that no nation should interfere in the internal affairs of another nation. The colonial powers constantly cited that principle when the United States was pressing for decolonization. In fact, the French and Portuguese gave it an elegant juridical underpinning by extending to some colonial possessions status as provinces of the metropole. Today we invoke the principle only when it serves our purpose.

Thus, the Ford administration made much of that injunction when Congress insisted on pressing the Soviet Union to permit more Jewish emigration; it was the Soviet Union's excuse for obduracy. Yet, now that the Soviets have agreed at Helsinki to liberalize their internal policies, our government is still not vigorously insisting on compliance with those commitments, this time because of its solicitude to preserve an illusory spirit of détente.

That the United Stoates uses the inhibition only when it suits our purposes is shown by our willingness to press South Africa to abandon the detestable practice of apartheid for a more civilized relation with its blacks and coloreds. In fact, we regularly ignore the principle of non-interference in most of our foreign aid transactions, and, if we are to avoid self-deception, we should admit at least to ourselves that we use it more often as a rationalization for action or inaction than a guide to policy.

These, then, are some of the factors that limit our country, both in pursuing the objective of survival and in encouraging individual freedom. Some result from the objective facts of the world scene—primarily the continued threat from a Soviet Union bent on exploiting any opportunity to expand its influence—some from wishful thinking, and some from an uncritical acceptance of slogans or assumptions that do not reflect reality. Often our reliance on these illusory elements is costly but not critical; yet if they encourage the compulsive single-minded pursuit of a misguided policy as they did in Vietnam, they can have tragic consequences.

Today, by far the most serious area of danger that might involve the superpowers in a major war is the Arab-Israeli struggle and, at the risk of making some observations with which many may disagree, I shall suggest how certain of the constraints I have enumerated threaten to paralyze American policy at a time when it is imperative that peace be urgently pursued.

Here we may do well to consult history. After the Congress of Vienna early in the nineteenth century, the major powers systematically took steps to settle local quarrels that seriously affected their interests, and it was only when their system broke down over a Balkan dispute that World War I finally came about. Their principal instrument for preventing the development of these areas of infection was that loose but reasonably effective device known as the Concert of Europe. Sometimes the methods used were direct and surgical, involving the landing of troops, as in Crete in 1896. But in most cases, once the great powers were in agreement on a solution, they could make it effective through diplomatic methods.

After World War I, the operative principle of the Concert of Europe, that the great powers should keep the peace by settling disputes, was institutionalized. Under the Covenant of the League of Nations, the task of bringing the great powers together for this purpose was assigned to the League Council. Later, under the Charter of the United Nations, the Security Council was given this responsibility. Unfortunately, the division of the world into two rival camps has so far prevented the Security Council from effectively carrying out its assigned role. But, up to now, we have been lucky, since local conflicts have, for the most part, taken place in areas of the world not of sufficient strategic interest to justify

superpower commitments of a kind that might lead to direct confrontation. In spite of the rhetoric with which our own government
sought to maintain support for its misconceived venture in Vietnam, the great powers involved in that conflict—the Soviet Union,
China, and the United States—all recognized that that struggle was
only a limited war. Nor did the tribal contest in Angola hold such
strategic implications that its outcome would seem to affect the
power balance in any material way.

But the Middle East is a different matter. Both geography and
geology combine to give it unique strategic significance, while, in
addition, America has a special sense of responsibility for the State
of Israel, stemming from history, a common concern for freedom
and the desire to help a gifted and valiant people realize an ancient
dream.

Yet, even though Secretary of State Kissinger said on several
occasions that he considered a final settlement of the Arab-Israeli
conflict impossible without Soviet cooperation, we have done little
to test the possibility that this is one area of conflict where the
superpowers might find a sufficient coincidence of interest to combine in seeking a settlement. So long as the Soviets can offer the
frontline Arab states the alternative of a possible military solution
by providing extensive supplies of advanced weapons, the chance
of a settlement seems extremely remote. Still, though no one can
prove it, there are reasons to believe that, if they were given a role
in the peace-making process, the Soviets might prove tractable.
Within recent years their experience in the Middle East has been
costly and disappointing. They suffered not only the loss of all the
arms they invested in Egypt, but also the humiliation of being
thrown out, while the weapons they continue to pour into Syria
and Iraq are received without much gratitude. Unquestionably
sensitive to the danger that another war might involve them in that
direct confrontation with the United States which they are assidu-
ously seeking to avoid, they have learned from experience that
they cannot control the impetuosity of their Arab clients.

With all the other problems that now confront them—the
menace of a hostile China and the disappointing performance of

their economy under pressure—they know that they must keep sufficiently friendly with the United States to assure a continued supply of equipment, technology and capital—to say nothing of the grain they require to meet shortfalls in their food production. Thus they might well be content to help quiet down the Middle East. After all, the Soviet Union did agree to Resolution 242 of the Security Council in 1967 which laid out very broad principles for a settlement and there is some basis for assuming that they might be prepared to concur in a detailed amplification of that resolution.

What has so far restrained a test of this hypothesis is not only our preference for keeping the Soviet Union out of the Middle East—a preference shared with Israel and with the more conservative Arab powers—but also the uncritical acceptance of certain of the assumptions and slogans I have already mentioned. For reasons I expounded above, I would dismiss the timeworn admonition against interfering in the internal affairs of the other countries as little more realistic than Secretary Stimson's justification for closing down our decoding operations after World War I on the ground that gentlemen do not read one another's mail. We interfere when it suits our purpose to do so.

But much more serious is our tacit acceptance of the belief that we must show special deference to the views of nations directly involved in local quarrels because they presumably understand the issues and can formulate policy better than we. In other words, we should not try to tell a foreign government what is good for its country, even though its action or inaction may jeopardize the peace of the area and, hence, the peace of the world. But this is no more valid than the dubious assumption I mentioned earlier that governments, whether of friendly or hostile states, can counted on to behave in a fashion that will contribute to the best long-range interests of their own countries. For quite understandable reasons, small nations involved in local quarrels necessarily focus their interests and attention so intensely on the quarrel itself that they tend to ignore the possible implications for great power conflict and world catastrophe. Every government that is in any sense responsive to democratic principles must live within its own national political environment, and if that government is based on an uneasy coalition—as is now the case with the Israeli government—it must avoid incisive actions that would alienate one faction or another. Where, as in Israel today, the government has only a miniscule majority in the parliament, it must necessarily shape its policy regarding a settlement with its Arab neighbors to reflect the lowest common denominator of opinion or—stated in realistic terms—the government cannot possibly risk initiatives in the search for peace that could be remotely regarded as major concessions.

Nor do the frontline Arab states have any greater freedom of action. Although President Assad of Syria has felt compelled to move against the PLO in order to prevent reckless acts that might precipitate a premature conflict with Israel, he would gravely endanger his own domestic position if he were to make serious concessions to Israel with regard to the Golan Heights or the Palestinian issue. Nor is King Hussein, sturdy as he has shown himself, sufficiently in control of the politics of the West Bank to be able to negotiate a Palestianian settlement. Finally, the rulers of Saudi Arabia, though obviously desirous of peace that would permit them to address themselves to the economic development of their country and the Arab world, must still live in an area surrounded by more activist Arab states, which imposes on them the need for substantial caution.

What all this adds up to is that neither the frontline Arab states nor Israel are in a position where the leaders dare make the concessions essential to a settlement without pressure from outside sources, even though some of those leaders might earnestly wish they could do so. Thus, I think it quite possible that many of those leaders might privately welcome external pressure that would compel them to do what they recognize as essential in the long–range interests of their countries, while relieving them of the onus of voluntarily taking unpopular actions.

It is late in the day and a further stalemate is extremely dangerous. The Sinai Agreement, which split Egypt from the rest of the Arab world, was no more than a tactical exercise to buy time, yet there is no indication that time is working on the side either of

Israel or of peace. On the contrary, so long as the critical problems of the area—the Palestinian issue, the Golan Heights, and Jerusalem—continue to fester while each side accumulates an increasing arsenal of more and more sophisticated weapons, the greater the danger that a new conflict may involve both the United States and the Soviet Union to such an extent as to create a serious threat of a direct confrontation. Moreover, another conflict would automatically be accompanied by a second, and this time probably a more far-reaching, oil embargo, at a time when America continues to increase its dependence on Arab oil.

Under these circumstances, the question of a more direct and vigorous American initiative must be critically reexamined, for it would be a mistake to assume that the troubles over Lebanon will permanently disrupt Arab unity. Can we afford to sit idly by while increasingly sophisticated arms pile up on both sides, Israel remains stretched to the breaking point as a garrison state, and the agonizing substantive problems of the area are left unresolved?

Although, as I have earlier suggested, the European powers of the nineteenth century recognized that the parties to local conflicts were often too estranged by history, fear, and passion to compromise their differences without outside help, the United States has been held back from taking a strong initiative by considerations that need careful rethinking. Among them has been the concern that great power political intervention might be condemned as an effort "impose a peace"—a phrase with such an abhorrent sound that even the member nations of the Concert of Europe persistently denied that they were ever imposing a peace, even when engaged in doing it. Yet just what does the phrase imply? In one sense, every peace is an imposed peace. Certainly the ambition of the more extreme elements on each side of the Arab-Israeli struggle is to bring about precisely that. The most radical Arabs would like to impose a peace by driving the Israelis into the sea; the more hawkish Israelis would like to impose a peace by freezing the boundaries that Israel achieved by force of arms in 1967—an effort, if continued, that seems to me almost certain to lead to a renewal of the fighting, but this time with far more lethal weapons.

Ideally, everyone would feel more comfortable with a settlement reached by the voluntary agreement of the parties, but I see no chance of that unless the parties are encouraged by firm outside guidance that would, in my view, require the laying out in advance of a detailed plan of settlement as the basis for negotiation. To bring that about we must not be put off by the dubious thesis that, while it is all right for peace to be imposed by one or the other of the parties—if it has the force of arms to do it—or even by an equilibium achieved through the play of force and counterforce, it must not be the work of outside powers, even though they may operate through the mechanism of the Security Council which was established precisely for that purpose. Obviously, the Security Council would not impose a peace by means of gunboats, as the Concert of Europe did in Crete toward the end of the nineteenth century. Its most effective sanction would be for both the Soviet Union and the Western powers to cut off the flow of arms into the area—a decision that would help to concentrate the minds of the parties on the plan of settlement supplied them as the basis for negotiation.

I have argued in the course of these comments that the Soviet Union might be willing to agree to a plan of settlement that represented an amplification of Resolution 242. Yet, though I think this might be the case, I certainly do not take it for granted. If the Soviet Union should not agree to a plan that was, in the American view, fair to all parties and that guaranteed the security of Israel beyond any question—and I wish to leave no ambiguity on that point—the United States should still present to the parties its own formulation of such a plan so as to provide something specific as the basis for a negotiation. For us to hesitate to take a firm initiative, while limiting ourselves to nibbling at little bits and pieces of the problem, seems to me an exercise in futility at a time when neither Israel nor the United States nor the world can afford further delay.

In the final analysis, the problem we Americans face is this: Can our country continue to withhold a serious effort to resolve the festering problems of the Middle East, out of deference to slogans and inhibitions and false assumptions which cannot stand critical examination, when the   continuance of those festering problems threatens, sooner or later, to bring about a resumption of fighting that would not only disable the West economically by bringing about a new oil embargo but—even more important—might create conditions in which the United States or the Soviet Union would feel compelled to intervene directly and thus set in motion forces that could precipitate a major confrontation?

If I have concentrated largely on the restrictive conditions under which we must seek to achieve the American purpose, I have done this deliberately. While it is relatively easy to determine what, in broad abstract terms, we would like to accomplish, that formulation will, it seems to me, have little meaning unless we look hard at the restrictions under which we must operate. Some of those restrictions result from objective facts of the world situation which we can do little to alter in the short term. Others are of our own making and we can liberate ourselves only if we have the will to disregard the habits of thought and pressures to which any government is necessarily subject.

I have emphasized the Middle East, both because it is a case study illustrating the fragile reasoning underlying certain of the restrictions and inhibitions that limit our freedom of action, but also because the area contains a ticking time bomb that can—and, if we do not act incisively, almost certainly will—explode with devastating consequences not merely for Israel and world oil supplies but for world peace, and even possibly world survival.

This is the most immediate danger we face, but, in the longer range, there are a vast array of problems which are terrifying to contemplate but which we must approach with firmer will than we have done in the past. Nuclear weapons will almost certainly proliferate to an alarming degree within the next decade, and anyone who now looks back over the past few years must be appalled at the laxity with which we have dealt with this problem. Almost equally important has been the recklessness with which we have spread conventional arms around the world. The time has long passed when we should stop trying to settle local quarrels by bribing the parties with sophisticated weapons or atomic reactors.

Meanwhile enormous problems are building up concerning

man's relations with nature, as well as with his fellow man: the problems of excessive population growth rates, the meeting of the world's food needs, the prospect of raw material stringencies, the problems of pollution, and so on.

It is a formidable agenda that cannot be met without strong American leadership. To get through the turbulent years ahead will test not merely the common sense, but the will and vigor of the American people. It will not be easy.

MARTIN E. MARTY

3.

THE CHANGING ROLE OF RELIGION IN AMERICAN SOCIETY

In 1776 the percentage of American colonists who were active church members was without doubt much lower than it was in 1976. Yet those who trace the roots of the Revolution can, with little difficulty, show how active was the public role of the religionists in the earliest days of "national purpose." Liberals and conservatives, northerners and southerners, otherworldly pietists and this-worldly preachers to merchants, establishmentarians and dissenters alike contributed rhetoric, ideas, and congregations to the colonists' cause. Many Loyalists, by the same token, contributed on religious grounds to the opposing cause. Yet, for all the religious celebration of the Bicentennial and all the religious reflections on the meaning of these two hundred years, in addressing the national purpose today it would be most difficult to bring to focus a specific role or formal function for religion.

The change has come about in part as a result of a change

from a premodern to a modern or postmodern situation. Whatever
the pre- and post- prefixes mean, the meanings include a trend
toward division of labor. The informal "modern pact" has allowed
religious institutions to minister to the private, familial, and lei-
sured sides of life while tending to exclude them increasingly from
the civil and public role. When Queen Isabella "got religion", there
were immediate public consequences. Her renewed Catholicism
led to aggression against the Moors, expulsion of Jews, and clarity
of purpose among explorers in the Western seas. When John Win-
throp made religious decisions, they had an impact on the civil life
of Massachusetts Bay. In 1976 presidential candidates could be re-
markably religious as the world defines religion, but they spent
most of their energy showing that their religious commitments
would have little impact on the world of policy and public decision.

The 1976 presidential election revealed how little institutional
bloc voting power was left in America's voluntary religious organizations. Ideology related to theology—as in the case of the abortion
question—could only with great difficulty and some embarrassment be introduced into public discussion. And there seemed to be
no civil counterparts to Benjamin Franklin, Thomas Jefferson, or
James Madison—professors of "the public philosophy," or what
Benjamin Franklin called "publick Religion"—who could bring
noninstitutional religious viewpoints to public attention.

This reversal of situations between 1776 and 1976 makes one
a bit diffident about relating religion to national purpose. But, then,
are other sectors of life contributing to the discussion of national
purpose? Is there such a discussion? Did the presidential candidates
do any more than ask a public to trust them to wire together the
old system a little longer, to lubricate its wheels, to keep it going?
Would we be better off were we assigned the topic "the changing
role of education" or media or economics or politics in the discussion of national purpose? On the assumption that such discussion
is rare and difficult today, we proceed rather with a different range
of ideas. These ideas are designed to help account for the present
situation, to see the choices behind it, the assets and liabilities
connected with it, and to look for signs of hope for a future more
lively engagement with national purpose. With that in mind, we

turn with some enthusiasm to an attempt to characterize religion in our current national adventure. To no one's surprise, difficulties will present themselves from the first word on.

"Anything anybody can say about America is true."[1] Emmett Grogan's comment may have been tinged with cynicism; it may have been evoked by awe. America has been shaped by so many colorful but contradictory influences that almost any proposition about the nation seems to be defensible. The field of religion illustrates this. The United States Supreme Court, the appointed guardian of America's secular legal tradition, has made the point that it has given "specific" recognition to the proposition that "[we] are a religious people whose institutions presuppose a Supreme Being."[2] America as a nation is secular and America is at the same time religious, yet most people have seen secular and religious to be opposed concepts.

So far as the nation's citizens themselves are concerned it remains difficult to generalize about the role of religion. To many, America is rich in spiritual belief and behavior, as evidenced by the presence of more than 300 religious groups listed in the *Yearbook of American and Canadian Churches.*[3] To just as many other observers, America has been a display case for old and even vulgar materialisms, as seen in the lust for power and possession on the part of its citizens. British sociologist David Martin, in the face of these extremes, propels on stage a single character who forces a revision of categories: "the Texan Baptist millionaire," who, says Martin, is devoted to the otherworldly spirituality of his Baptist church and equally devoted to this–worldly materialism of his millionairedom. According to him, this man "would not necessarily fix his eye singly and solely on the appropriation of deferred benefits."[4] Americans are spiritual and materialist, although most people have seen "spiritual" and "materialist" to be in opposition to each other.

So diverse and diffuse are the American experiences that it is tempting for analysts to retreat into the safe generalization that the only thing to be said about religion in American society is that it happens in a place called America. As Arthur H. Robinson and Barbara Bartz Petechnik remind us in a book on mapping, "Every-

thing is somewhere, and no matter what other characteristics ob-
jects do not share, they always share relative location, that is, spa-
tiality. . . . "⁵ We need not be content with this minimal definition,
however. American religions help shape and are shaped by their
culture. It is possible to discern some broad outlines, some macro--
trends in the field of religious change in this two hundred-year-old
nation.

Not everything in it is utterly changed; there are continuities.
For example, religion here as elsewhere seems always to have had
to do with meaning, belonging, and purpose in life. The changes
we shall discuss occur in the context of those continuous themes.
The specific meanings, belongings, and purposes are the elements
of change. When one associates these themes with religion, some
boundaries are necessary, since not all search for meaning, belonging, and purpose has to be called "religious."

Sometimes the boundaries are drawn too narrowly. A habit
shared by broad publics and some specialized social scientists
sometimes restricts religion only to that which is monitored by
traditional and formal institutions. Say that a fifty-year-old man
was dropped off for his weekly spiritual pit stop at a Protestant
Sunday School forty years earlier. There, presumably, he was giv-
en whatever formal dose of religious meaning he was ever to find,
since he has not darkened church doorways since. A Jew experienced the rite of passage called "bar mitzvah" and has never
showed up at the synagougue for a high holy day since. It is often
assumed that these men stopped being religious in adolescence. A
woman born in a Greek Orthodox Church family once participated
in charities organized through that church. Through them she was
supposed to have focused her religious purpose in life. Did her
religion come to an end when she broke her ties? Obviously these
institutional boundaries are too constricting to describe life as lived
in America.

On the other hand, some anthropologists and theologians enjoy making the boundaries so extensive that they seem coextensive
with life itself. Then one must ask, "If everything is religious, is
anything religious?" Such scholars consider as religious all attempts by anyone to be truly serious and intense about life. An-

thropologist Clifford Geertz has fallen victim to such imperialism because of some of the uses to which his definition of religion is put. He says a religion is:

(1) a system of symbols which act to
(2) establish powerful, pervasive and long-lasting moods and motivations in men by
(3) formulating conceptions of a general order of existence and
(4) clothing these conceptions with such an aura of factuality that
(5) the moods and motivations seem uniquely realistic.[6]

Since the rites of professional football, the American Legion, the Masons, the Little League, Weight Watchers, and the American academic convocations all bear many of these marks, each of them can be and all of them probably have been described as the *real* religion of millions—even if these millions are also devoted and deep Jews, Catholics, or Protestants and therefore associated with other profound traditional "systems of symbols."

Wary as one may be of such misuses of Geertz, it is at the same time valid to use his approach to enlarge the conventionally narrowed scope of institutional definition. That Sunday school alumnus may today be obsessed with the vision of seer Edgar Cayce or may be such a devotee of the yogi at his friendly neighborhood YMCA that these attachments fill the place in his life that historic church religion did for his parents. The survivor of the bar mitzvah may now so heartily find his ultimate concern in the symbol system of secular Zionism or the Fellowship of Reconciliation that a serious observer must speak of these as his religion. And that Greek Orthodox woman may have later joined the John Birch Society or its competitors, organizations that invoke and impose complex and burdening symbol systems that are more effective for defining meaning, belonging, and purpose, than are most churches.

Somewhere between the act of restricting religion to institutions and broadening it to match the whole human condition lie the definitions appropriate to religion in American society. John Stuart Mill's advice is a minor stay, at least, against mere chaos and confusion: "Above all, to insist on having the meaning of a word clearly understood before using it, word and the meaning of a proposition before assenting to it; these are the lessons we learn from ancient dialecticians."[7] Ancient dialecticians may not be satisfied with the result, but I hope they would welcome an effort to give a brief description of what this historian, at least, looks for when defining or discerning American religion.

If several of the following six elements are present, I tend to give attention and be alert to the religious dimensions of a subject. First what Paul Tillich called "ultimate concern" must be present. If one's search for meaning in synagogue leaves him satisfied with proximates, the observer pushes and probes further to find where it is that an individual locates that which concerns him or her ultimately. Second, normally—though, as we shall see, for many Americans, decreasingly—this concern is grasped communally, in the company of others who share the same vision or purpose. Third, one tends to speak of religion when these communal concerns are embodied in myths and symbols, when speech and expression are not always reduced to the most abstract forms but appear in time-sanctioned and evocative or emotive forms. Fourth, rites and ceremonies, attempts to render formal and repetitive the celebration of these myths and symbols, lead us again to reach for the term "religious." Next, one looks for suggestions that behind the current drama there is a larger transaction, a metaphysical or quasimetaphysical backdrop or argument. Finally, behavioral correlates and consequences flow: one acts out the religion through patterns of ethics and conduct, manners and morals, diets, and disciplines.[8]

The combinations are what matter. Not all rites need be religious, nor are all metaphysical explanations or patterns of conduct. Taken together they alert us to speak of something as religious. With these spectacles, then, we are ready to look at the changing role of religion in American society.

Two Perceptions, Two Locations

The idea that "anything anybody can say about America is true," the disturbing comment with which we began, can be qualified to some extent if we perceive American religionists and their observers as sharing fundamentally one of two principal locations or fields of perception. Picture the United States as a great building, a Pentagon or Versailles Palace or mazeway, full of both chambers or compartments and broad corridors. American citizens see or experience religion differently depending upon whether their primary locations are the symbolic chambers or the corridors. Commuters between the two lead necessarily confusing and often creative lives: they are a distinct minority.

The chambered or compartmented version is the form religion takes for the great majority of the pious, the mainstream of "middle" Americans. They would belong to a denomination whose Friday or Sunday worship folders include calendars that depict or prescribe most rhythms of their religious life. Birth, rites of adolescence, marriage, and death; the patterns of the day, week, and year; the systems of symbol and status are all determined by the religious institution. This is a world hardly remembered and seldom experienced by many "corridor" people in the academy or the field of mass communications. They may go slumming or field tripping on occasion, but they do not live in the compartments.

A glance at today's map shows how durable these separate zones or fields of perception and belonging can be.[9] Far from being a merely mobile, blurring, religiously pluralist society, America remains in its two hundredth year a collection of regions in which one or another religion tends to predominate in most counties. According to recent statistical surveys and corollary efforts at mapping, the United States retains five such large compartmentalized regions in which one religion outnumbers and outinfluences all others. The solid South remains solidly Baptist. In many a middle-sized southern city one can go through life knowing little social contact with any non-Baptist, and never meeting a Jew, an Eastern Orthodox Christian, or even a Roman Catholic. The "border state" zone from Maryland west to Kansas has a strong though not an overwhelming Methodist regional sense. The upper Midwest provides huge territories for Lutheran enclaves. Utah is a Mormon empire. The tips of Texas, Louisiana, and Florida; all of California, the entire northeast and the Great Lakes industrial riviera, are dominated by Catholics though, given the urban condition in most of these places, Catholics share space with Jews and black Protestants in cities, white Protestants in suburbs and many other faiths and forces in general.

Within these regions, compartments further survive in the form of ghettos, wards, and even suburbs where economic stratifications or joint migrations provide self-contained religious worlds. These are often reinforced by strong racial or ethnic bonds. Where the region or neighborhood do not provide clear compartments, people can fashion their own complete worlds-within-worlds and worldviews-within-worldviews. Some of these may be extremely mobile people. Jehovah's Witnesses who live in trailers and build interstate highways are typical. They have been everywhere but are able to stay with their kind. Their perceptions are filtered through their communal experience. Young Protestant conservatives may transfer from campus to campus. But the milieux of the University of Alabama, South Dakota State and Stanford have less impact on their conscious religion than might the portable and pervasive Campus Crusade organization that fashions for them a virtual cocoon of meanings, a web of belongings, a focus for purpose.

People are in a compartment because they were born there and it is still part of their reflexive outlook or because they chose to go and maybe even to flee there, in which case it becomes an intentional and reflective element. Did any sociologist of 1966 foresee that by 1976 America's young would have spent much of the intervening decade being "anything but secular," finding new religious intensities in various forms of the counter culture, in Hassidic Jewish cells, in Catholic Pentecostal groupings, in Protestant Jesus and Pentecostal clusterings, in Hare Krishna and the Unification Church, and a thousand Eastern, occult, or therapeutic cults or cells? The observers and projectors of 1966 tended to move through the secular corridors. They did not see how many religious compartments remained satisfying to millions; how many that were still half-filled were ready to be filled again; how many new ones were being built.

Religion in those years acquired new and changing roles for

many citizens who had, as it were, been in the corridors, or who were able to shift from one chamber to another. One attempt to explain this phenomenon derives from the psychological approach having to do with peoples' search for boundaries and identity. Thus Robert Jay Lifton points to two factors, the sense of *"histori-cal, or psychohistorical* dislocation," a breaking in old nourishing traditions and symbols, and the *"flooding of imagery"* produced by the flow of mass communications and similar influences. Some of those that we have called corridor people cope with and even cele-brate these changes, but others react with "the closing off of iden-tity, the constriction of self-process, to a straight-and-narrow spe-cialization in psychological as well as in intellectual life, and to reluctance to let in any extraneous influence."[10] They move from corridors to denominational or cultic chambers, and then take on new perceptions in their new location.

People who inherit life in the chambers may perceive reality in a different way than do those who choose to walk corridors. The former regard religious symbols with what Paul Ricoeur calls "primitive naïveté," uncritically and without knowing or being able seriously to entertain other symbol systems, worldviews, or even institutional arrangements.[11] The Oklahoma child born into the Church of Christ is not tempted to join a Hare Krishna group, about which she never hears, or hears only with negative refer-ence. "He who never visits thinks his mother is the only cook," say the Bantu in Africa.[12] It is still possible to do little physical or psychic visiting, even in mobile and media-saturated America.

The move from chamber to chamber may, however, mean a move toward "a second naïveté," in which as Ricoeur describes it "by *interpreting* . . . we can *hear* again." Such is the approach of the believer-critic. But other people may change to new chambers, as a generation makes strenuous attempts to reenter the world of primitive naïveté. A person is "into" Nichiren Shoshu one year, "into" Transcendental Meditation the next, "into" Jews for Jesus the next, and fundamentalisms a year later. Such efforts to acquire a tradition or reconstruct lost worldviews seem pathetic to many observers. Al Ghazali centuries ago said, "There is no hope of re-turning to a traditional faith after it has once been abandoned,

since the essential condition in the holder of a traditional faith is
that he should not know he is a traditionalist"[13] Yet an Al Ghazali
could not have anticipated how arduous such efforts would have to
be in a place like pluralist America at a time when the search for
boundaries and identities is intense. On the other hand, the large
and growing American minority that inhabits psychic or spiritual
corridors or mazeways is aware of the existence of many chambers
and corridors in this nation. But rather than retreat into one, a
member is likely to remain the critic, the analyst, the observer, the
voyeur, or at most, the eclectic and half-engaged participant in any
religious group.

In the spring of 1976 the two worlds of corridor and chamber
came together when northern academicians and New York media
people began to have to make sense of the relatively intact chambered world of Plains, Georgia. One newsweekly editior told me
that no one in her office could picture the Democratic candidate as
being spiritually authentic because of the way he talked about
Jesus, was a deacon, taught Sunday School, and claimed to have
been "born again." "No one in our office ever met anyone who
ever met anyone who claimed to have been 'born again.' "

The commuter between these worlds can be well-poised to
recognize the conflict of perceptions and locations in his or her own
personal experience. The priest-anthropologist at a major university on Sunday wears a collar and immerses himself in the life of
an ordinary Catholic parish, perhaps in an Italian ward where the
compartmental style survives somehow. But to his weedkay university colleagues, he "blends into the woodwork" of the faculty
club, goes about his field work and writing the same way whether
or not God exists or the transcendent order impinges on the field of
research. Seldom do the people of his two different worlds meet.
The high church Episcopalian physicist shares in and enjoys a pre-
fabricated world at Eucharist, and then fabricates a world rich in
other kinds of explanations and intentions with her colleagues.

The long-term trends suggest that more and more Americans
will move from secure compartments to the corridors and connect-
ing worlds. The media long ago invaded the chambers of the mon-

asteries. The Jesus people adopted the status world of athletics and the world of what they used to call "fleshly lust" by favoring "Jocks for Jesus" and the impulse to have Miss America testify to her born-again experience. The Texan Baptist millionaire's personal synthesis may not be easily transmitted to a new generation. Intermarriage across religious lines leads toward new confusions and commutations. Both in the prosperity of affluent society and the devastation of the Okies' world back in the time of the *Grapes of Wrath,* mobility made the act of traditioning a difficult matter to sustain. Still, counterefforts are fervent. Shall we see significance in the fact that seven of the eight least "churched" states in America are the western ones, the last to be settled and the enduring symbols of mobility—Hawaii, Alaska, California, Oregon, Washington being among them? And that most of these, California in particular, are the proverbial and actual homes of many new attempts at compartmentalizing the "new religions," the Eastern, occult, and therapeutic groups of the recent past?

Over against the "constrictive" type of chambered religion, there has emerged what Lifton calls the Protean form which is "characterized by an interminable series of experiments and explorations, some shallow, some profound, each of which can readily be abandoned in favor of still new, psychological questions" among people who can tolerate what Eric Erikson calls "identity diffusion."[14] The Protean style is attractive to corridor people in their religious strivings. Thus Harvard's Harvey Cox has been both a theorist and activist of the Protean celebration. "The symbolic treasures of the full sweep of human history are available to us," he says, "everything from the oldest cave drawing to the newest image of Utopian hope."

British sociologist Bryan Wilson reckons with the fact that Cox and other "corridor" analysts see in this symbolic explosion not a threat to traditional religion but an emphasis that helps appropriate it in a new synthesis. "There are sociologists who profess to see in the growth of new cults important evidence that controverts the hypothesis that has become known as 'the secularization thesis'. For them, the new cults represent religious revival." Wilson, however, sees them as "a confirmation of the process of secularization.

They indicate the extent to which religion has become inconse-
quential for modern society." Here the American phrase "the religion of your choice" has reached its "highest expression in the
many new groups, but they reduce religion to the significance of
pushpin, poetry, or popcorn. They have no real consequence for
other social institutions, for political power structures, for technological constraints and controls. They add nothing to any prospective reintergration of society, and contribute nothing toward the
culture by which a society might live." Past religious revivals had
"significant social consequences." But in the world of our competing compartments and amazing mazeways "religious teaching and
practice can[not] exercise formative influence over whole societies,
or any significant segment of them."[15]

If Wilson is correct our corridored world in its current religious searching points to a dramatic change in the role of religion
in the whole American society. But just as the people he criticizes
too easily relish evidence against "the secularization thesis," it is
possible that he may not be alert to the emergence of a new junc-
ture or junctioning that might be called a kind of "religio–secular
society" where society is influenced in subtler, new ways, by the
new private religious groupings. Wilson's words are a valid caution
against those who claim that a whole new style of religious consciousness pervades and is being poised to reshape our culture,
thanks to the prosperity of some of the compatments of religion,
the newer evangelicalism, pentecostalism, Eastern faiths, and spiritual therapies.

Two Tendencies, Two Changed Roles

What people in the spiritual and institutional chambers of
American religion view only negatively, if they are aware of it at
all, is a great cultural shift that threatens them. I refer to a persistent trend from *institutional to invisible* religion. This present thesis in part calls into question the second of my six marks of religion, the communal dimension. If communality has been integral
to all definitions in the history of religion, this macro–trend may

portend a drastic shift in American, Western, and human religiosity in general. To establish the idea that in our century there is indeed a movement away from institutional religion as normative and even all-inclusive, it is necessary to take a backward glance to see whence we have come.

Institutional religion is not necessarily a part of the human condition, integral to all definitions of human social life at all times and in all places. It appeared at a certain moment and characterizes what might be called a stage in history. In many definitions of "primitive" religion there was little or no differentiation or separation of religious institutions, just as there were no clear spheres analogous to today's concepts of "sacred" and "secular." A long tradition of religious social analysis by people who remembered the chambers but inhabited the corridors sees the differentiation of religious institutions itself as a gift or blight of modernity. Thus John Murray Cuddihy summarizes the lineage of sociologist Talcott Parsons. He sees

> differentiation [as] the cutting edge of the modernization process, sundering cruelly what tradition has joined; . . . it separates church from state (the Catholic trauma), ethnicity from religion (the Jewish trauma). . . .Differentiation slices through ancient primordial ties and identities, leaving crisis and "wholeness hunger" in its wake.[16]

Doctor and witchdoctor parted, the weatherman left the shrine and entered the university or television studio. The priest no longer was believed to have enough control over the weather to assure a good day for the Sunday School picnic, to say nothing of a good crop. The cleric who today sips Sunday noon champagne and then blesses the fishing fleet or hounds is seen to be, at best, quaint.

The division of labor in religion occurred in America as the old Spanish and then English theocracies broke down, as church and state were separated, as religious institutions occupied a special social role in a voluntary society. These institutions live on, some of them with renewed potency, in the chambers of American society.

But these religious institutions have little impact on the corridors or the whole building. A "born-again" President is expected to be "President of all the people." What he believes in private life, he must assure us, will not be imposed upon all the people or ever invoked in their presence. Even when he uses the White House as his "bully pulpit" and speaks in cadences of our "publick Religion," he is in some ways a sectarian of civic faith. The Jehovah's Witnesses will not accept his theologizing, nor will most of the people at synagogue or mass take his religious proclamations seriously in centering their own meaning, belonging, and purpose in life. In turn, he and his congressional counterparts will not automatically respond to the many competing testimonies of the vestigial religious "blocs" from the compartments of life. The "abortion issue" and the "issue of support for Israel" in the 1976 campaign demonstrated the residual potency of religious or quasi-religious concerns, but these issues did not dominate in national politics or in shaping the whole society.

We are arguing that the modernizing, differentiating, or specializing process has now begun to move citizens even beyond traditional institutions into the private and, hence, "invisible" realm. British sociologist Michael Hill well describes what we now see to be the changing role of American religion:

> Instead of religion's function being that of a primary source of legitimation for the whole of society, it becomes increasingly a matter of private choice, restricted to the sphere of religiously interested participations. As a consequence of this process religion loses its public role, and as a corollary society looks elsewhere for the source of its authority.[17]

Thomas Luckmann, who has the patent on the phrase "invisible religion," speaks of a trend that he first discerned in late-industrial and "post-modern" Europe but which is spreading in America today:

> The social forms of religion emerging in modern industrial societies is characterized by the direct accessibility of the sacred cosmos, more precisely, of an assortment of religious themes, which makes religon today essentially a phenomenon of the "private sphere." The emerging social form of religion thus differs significantly from older social forms of religion which were characterized either by the diffusion of the sacred cosmos through the institutional structure of society or through institutional specialization of religion.[18]

This means that in the religion of the high-rise apartment and the long weekend, the world of the academy and mass media, the primary and secondary associations of life no longer confirm the values that were associated with meaning, belonging, and purpose when these were under the custodianship of religious institutions that had traditional weight and power. Religion becomes entirely a consumer affair, a matter of competing markets, something that cannot be checked out in the experience of others not in one's group. It has little meaning beyond one's own private chamber or, at best, beyond the slightly open compartment of one's choice.

The American participation in this trend was obscured or postponed for a time after midcentury by a religious revival that took the form of institution-building, in an age of prosperity and in a time in which people wanted to "sink down roots." It was further obscured by the momentary assertions of religious power on a social scale in the 1960s by the Second Vatican Council participants and the social activist elites in American religion. After these movements passed their peak, it was seen that most of the children of the suburban synagogue had not joined the temples' "alumni associations," that mainline churches no longer prospered in relation to their clienteles or decisively shaped the larger culture. The religions that did prosper, apart from the areas where huge religious complexes still dominated a region as in Utah or the South, did little to counter the differentiating trend when it was taken to its new extreme. The "Jews for Jesus," by proselytizing a young Jew, or Campus Crusaders, by raiding the more relaxed campus religious communities for recruits, further sunder youths' ties to traditional communities. They focus their positive work on such constrictive and specialized purposes that their converts cannot have the shaping role in relation to society that Michael Hill, Bryan Wilson, and others saw in the religion of the past.

This reduction of religion from the social to the private or from the institutional to the invisible spheres is partly compensated for by a parallel trend. America is seeing a change from *conventional to intentional religion.* This is the positive side of the "market" or "clientele" relation just described. By conventional we refer to reflexive, automatic attachment to the meaning, belonging, and purposive elements of inherited institutions and traditions. It would be naive for a religious historian to suggest that this is a wholly new trend. The process is a quarter of a millennium old in

America, for its roots derive from the largely Protestant "Great Awakening" of the 1730s and 1740s. In the Awakening the colonists saw the beginnings of the end of pure territorialism in religion at a time when individuals were summoned to "get religion" through conversion and group association. The American Revolution with its corollary religious events—including the rise of the distinction between civil and religious realms, or the "separation of church and state"—furthered the process by removing establishment or privileged place from the status of major religious institutions.

The Awakening and the Revolution were so successful that those who "got religion" were able for a time to further religion's social consequences through reformist churches and agencies that were, at first, voluntary and competitive, and thus "intentional," too. But soon these churches became virtually reestablished in the geographical regions we have already described, or they were established in the ethos and mores where they had been disestablished by law. It is safe to say that the typical American child who did not physically move away from the parental region or neighborhood in those years ordinarily found the parental religion to be inescapable. Escape, in any case, would have implied rebellion and often a move away from this area. The Great Jehovah or at least Aunt Marie was always looking down from the balcony to see whether the adolescent was in the church pew. Parents had no difficulty deciding what values to pass on in the context of Iowa Methodism, Boston Irish Catholicism, or the Orthodox Judaism of Irving Howe's *The World of Our Fathers*. This is not the moment to criticize or regret the parental values and the modes of transmission, but merely to point to their relative intactness.

In recent years religion has simply become more escapable than ever before. The locks, we might say, are off the chambers. The corridors are attractive. The shift of devotees from compartment to compartment, one which is so easy to make in a day of mass evangelism and group pressures, leaves habitual or conventional religion an increasing rarity. But if participants are not engaged by convention, with the result that they can easily drift off— witness losses in Catholicism since Vatican II or in the mainline

Protestant churches during the past fifteen years or so—those who *do* choose to participate are signalling their intentions and intentionality. They want to be saved, or to save. They have some theological questions, some personal anxiety, some altruistic impulse, some search for identity which, unlike their grandparents, they are free to take elsewhere than to religious centers of meaning, belonging, and purpose. Yet, not only do many "old-timers" stay around, but new people show up in these zones of intention.

"Less is more" has become the virtual motto of many religious leaders who, in the day of movement from institutional to invisible religion, welcome the counter-trend of the move from conventional to intentional faith. They expect to see institutional declines over the long decades and remain unimpressed by the short-term gains, however dramatic, of the constrictive or expresssive groups of today. The question for those who want to see religion have a bearing on the whole society is; How can these intentions be expressed again in the spheres of politics, public interpretation, the arts, and the like? Religious expression will not be potent in the old ways but in the eyes of such leadership it need not be impotent.

The Market and Changing Roles

"The market" may seem to be a crude and unspiritual term for describing the place of today's transactions between religious compartments and corridors. But it can also be seen as a relatively neutral term, appropriate for the realization that in the society we have discerned as emergent, the religion that does not meet manifest or easily recognizable needs will tend to fossilize and dwindle. David Kaplan reduces this tendency and its opposite to the forces of a natural law in what he calls the Law of Cultural Dominance. "That cultural system which more effectively exploits the energy resources of a given environment will tend to spread in that environment at the expense of less effective systems."[19] It is possible to see the various competing clusters in American religion—evangelical-fundamentalist Protestantism, mainline Protestantism-Catholicism-Judaism, "publick" or civil religion, the new religions, racial and ethnic religious clusters, Pentecostalism, and the like—as "cultural systems." At least, they are subcultures or subsystems competing to fill the society's many ecological nooks and crannies with their various offerings.[20]

Those religious groups that prosper at the expense of others often do so by advertising that they are working against the zeitgeist, the spirit of the times. But in fact, they turn out to be addressing it, working within its context, and then contributing to reinforcing it and the formal system it generates. In this light, it is important to point to some short-term trends that may have long-range significance. We have less confidence in them than in the macro-tendencies described above. Yet it is impossible to be responsible about "the changing role of religion in America" without making at least brief concluding reference to them. American religion is a game played by innings, and we shall look now at the current inning. Two major impulses appeared in the recent past and will probably remain for some time to come.

The first is a trend toward *immediacy* in religion. The religion that prospers relies less patently on conventional and inherited institutions, elaborate bureaucracies, rationalized styles of administration, or modes of organization that are experienced as unresponsive. Tom Wolfe speaks of the seventies as the "Me Decade,"[21] and prosperous religions immediately address this "Me." Now, it is not likely that primitive or historic faiths would have long survived had they not met "my" needs, but they did so in the context of long and tested traditions that at least gave the impression of existing durably apart from the year's psychological needs. In a time when people seek authority for definition but therapy for what ails them or experience when they are "wholeness-hungry," the religious systems that concentrate on the experiential elements prosper. People want to be "born again," to have a spiritual "kick" or "high," to be Gracious Losers in the world of religious weight watchers, to relate religion to health foods and T-groups, ecstasy and enthusiasm, and to know "the immediate experience" at the expense of theory.

At this moment the suggestion that religion has social dimensions or that religious groups over the long pull have to out-think others in their environment would have little market effect or appeal, however integral to the professed faiths such claims might be. This is not the inning or the decade, say the successful religionists, to be assertive in activist or intellectual ways. Meaning, belonging, and purpose characteristically are sought and found in today's American cultures, be they secular or religious, apart from such styles of acting and thinking. At its worst, the prevailing trend may produce spiritual hedonism and narcissism. At its best, it sees religion addressing the legitimate need for healing and spiritual experiences to which classic religions addressed thmselves.

The second, current trend has to do with the organization of these religious impulses, and involves movement from the universal toward the *particular*. After a middle third of a century devoted to United Nations, World Councils of Churches, Vatican Councils, and ecumenical movements, social religion in America today reorganizes itself around smaller social units: the nation, the denomination, the ethnic–religious cluster, the sect. Women define themselves over against men in religion; the generations claim, or claimed, to have qualitatively different experiences of the spiritual; "black theology" is but one code word for the many racial–ethnic–tribal particularities. The local synagogue or church preempts most attention and support.

Such tendencies can be and, I am ready to say, are creative protests against technology or politics when these diminish the human and the local. They at least allow for local responsiveness and initiative in the neglected realms of religious social engagement or systematic religious thought. As a reaction they are understandable to people; as a mode of being they point to something durably valuable in human contexts.

But American discourse is not only determined locally and in competing particular cells. There are also symbols appealing to masses, networks that connect such symbols, governmental agencies that coerce assent to them on at least modest scales. As creative protest localism has been a delight to many, but as an inclusive expression, it is a troubling irony that a nation whose motto is *E Pluribus Unum* should have spent the decade leading up to its Bicentennial celebrating, also in religion, the idea of *Ex Uno Plures*.

What I have just pointed to may be only the momentary trend of "this half of the inning." It would be foolish for religious leaders to retool themselves and to reorient institutions so that they meet what may only be the obsessive concerns of the present, denying elements that are integral to their traditions, constitutive parts of what they must through the years offer in the way of meaning, belonging, and purpose.

What is the "non-religious" corridor person to make of the trends? Paradoxically, the more the current styles of religion prosper, the less likely is the corridor person to be inconvenienced by them. One may need to push aside a Hare Krishna representative in the airport or show the door to Jehovah's Witnesses or Jews for Jesus. One may have to turn the knob quickly past televised mass evangelism in search of an old film, or curse one's fate if taken captive by religious broadcasting on a Sunday morning in a lonely motel room. Now and then it may be necessary to walk to the nearest trash barrel to deposit the tract just imposed upon one. Only now and then are there reasons to be alert and possibly fearful. Many Americans are concerned lest the right-wing politics of "born-again" Christian Embassy people in Washington upset the historic terms of participation in American secular political life. Some are nervous about the possibility that any growth in numbers or wealth of the Unification Church might lead toward a style of messianic Korean anti-Communism in an American caught off-guard.

More positively, many of the nonreligious, if they are humane, are quite content to see the religion of the day offer meaning, belonging, and purpose in at worst harmless and often quite positive ways. People moved by these impulses overcome loneliness in nursing homes. They engage in works of love through parish and synagogue. They produce a generation of young people who at least don't create problems of delinquency and who at best often find astonishing resources for serving others. They minister to the lonely and abandoned and provide a center for affirmation. They make contributions to middle-range institutions like family and voluntary association and thus help transmit something valuable and valid in traditions. To the nonreligious, not only can the religious claimants and adherents not all be "true"—they are not even that to themselves—they all may even be perceived as "false." So in terms of philosophical neatness the nonreligious might like to see the religious become more enlightened, less held in thrall. But on the scale of concerns that exercise them, most Americans have learned the value of not disrupting the systems of meaning, belonging, and purpose of others.

In a strange sense, the "more religious" that people and their clusterings become—as people usually define "religious"—the less religious they are in reference to the whole society. They are more dismissible. When apolitical religion or atheological faith–systems encounter the political and theological arenas, they may begin to look less religious and more secular, as people usually define secular. But there they can both inconvenience others and offer some threat or promise to the larger society. Mohandas Gandhi, Martin Luther King, Jr., Mother Teresa, Dorothy Day, Abraham Joshua Heschel, Alexander Solzhenitsyn and their kin and kind have probed their religious traditions and communities to their depths. From their particular visions they have come nearer to the universal, reminding us that the religious genius or prophet, rare in any day, can quicken social movements in our own time. They seem to violate all the perceptions and preconceptions we nurture in our chambers and corridors.

The combination of immediacy and particularism can contribute in many valid ways to personal religion. In a difficult world, there are few reasons to try to remove any of the comforts, challenges, or solaces that issue from such faith. But by themselves the current accents keep us from developing anew what might be called a "public theology." We lack John Deweys or Walter Lippmanns who, from the public side, talk their kind of secular theology, public philosophy, or what Dewey called A Common Faith. My present concern, however, is the silence from the formal religious camp. We lack figures, great or small, who successfully speak out of specific theological traditions to address the public weal as did Reinhold Niebuhr, John Courtney Murray, and Abraham Joshua Heschel out of Protestant, Catholic, and Jewish resources as recently as ten years ago. One does not invent genius or produce great figures such as these. But a religious public can create itself as an audience or even a custodian of values that can be transmitted and transformed by such public theologians.

Today we look, then, for more activity between the zone of completely individualistic "invisible religion" and mass bureaucracy or unresponsive bigness in government and the major institutions of life. In that zone the local movement, cell, parish, synagogue, church, interest group, or congregation has come to show a potential for new life. Social critics include these with families, voluntary associations, schools, and other bearers of tradition and values as agencies or institutions deserving special attention these years. If we are a *communitas communitatum*, a community of communities, the lives of these subcommunities can have public roles. There meanings are refined, words rehearsed; caring in such intimate sectors can be a parable or a goad to action in a wider world. If the people in such groups overcome selfish concerns, look for networks within which to connect and discern common symbols, it is possible that they can counter some of the anomie and apathy of the times. At the very least, without tempting anyone to utopianism, they would be an alternative to fashionable cynicism or despair. They could be part of a beginning of a renewed engagement between religion and the discussion of national purpose that we need today and might welcome tomorrow.

Notes

1. Quoted in Art Spiegelman and Bob Schneider, *Whole Grains: A Book of Quotations* (New York: Douglas Links, 1973), p. 52.
2. This dictum from Zorach v. Clauson, 343 U. S. 306, 313 (1952) is quoted in Abington School District v. Schempp (1963); see Arthur B. Frommer, ed., *The Bible and the Public Schools* New York: Affiliated Publishers, 1963), p. 52.
3. The *Yearbook of American and Canadian Churches* most recent edition is edited by Constant H. Jacquet, Jr. (New York and Nashville: Abingdon Press, 1976).
4. David Martin, "Toward Eliminating the Concept of

Secularization," in Julius Gould, ed., *Penguin Survey of the Social Sciences 1965* (Baltimore: Penguin, 1965), p. 171.

5. Arthur H. Robinson and Barbara Bartz Petchenik, *The Nature of Maps* (Chicago: University of Chicago Press, 1976), p. 44.

6. Clifford Gertz, "Religion as a Cultural System," in Donald Cutler, ed., *The Religious Situation: 1968* (Boston: Beacon Press, 1968), p. 643.

7. Quoted by Robinson and Petchenik, *Maps*, p. 1.

8. For an elaboration, see Martin E. Marty, *A Nation of Behavers* (Chicago: University of Chicago Press, 1976), pp. 33f.

9. Douglas W. Johnson, Paul R. Picard, and Bernard Quinn, *Churches and Church Menbership in the United States* (Washington, D. C.: Glenmary Research Center, 1974).

10. Robert Jay Lifton, *Boundaries: Psychological Man in Revolution* (New York: Vintage, 1970), pp. 43, 51.

11. Paul Ricoeur, *The Symbolism of Evil* (New York: Harper and Row, 1967), p. 351.

12. Quoted by John V. Taylor, *The Primal Vision* (Philadelphia: Fortress, 1964), p.26.

13. Quoted by Ernest Gellner, *Legitimation of Belief* (Cambridge: Cambirdge University Press, 1974), p. 147.

14. Lifton, *Boundaries*, p. 44.

15. Cox is quoted by Bryan Wilson, *Contemporary Transformations of Religion* (London: Oxford University Press, 1976), p. 93; Wilson's argument cited here is on p. 95f.

16. John Murray Cuddihy, *The Ordeal of Civility: Freud, Marx, Levi-Strauss, and the Jewish Struggle with Modernity* (New York: Basic Books, 1974), pp. 234, 9, 10.

17. Michael Hill, *A Sociology of Religion* (New York: Basic Books, 1973), pp. 228ff.

18. Thomas Luckmann, *The Invisible Religion* (New York: Macmillan, 1967), p. 103.

19. David Kaplan, "The Law of Cultural Dominance," chapter 4 in Marshall D. Sahlins *et al.*, *Evolution and Culture* (Ann Arbor: Unviersty of Michigan Press, 1960), p. 1975

20. For a discussion of these clusters see Marty, *A Nation of Behavers.*

21. Tom Wolfe, "The 'Me' Decade and the Third Great Awakening," *New York Magazine*, 9 (34):26-40.

BARRY COMMONER

4.

A NEW HISTORIC PASSAGE: ENERGY, THE ECONOMY, AND THE ERA OF CONSTRAINTS

THE UNITED STATES is on the verge of a new historic passage. Once seen as a place almost infinitely rich in land and resources, now the nation confronts resource limitations and environmental degradation. Once capable of producing enough wealth to sustain a rising standard of living and rapid growth, now the nation is entering an era of constraints.

This historic transition is already apparent in the economic effects of the new constraints. Nearly all of our present energy sources are nonrenewable, and exhibit the earliest manifestation of the law of diminishing returns—an exponential increase in price. In turn, rising energy prices have intensified inflation and eroded living standards. Much of the increased demand for energy is due to the introduction of production technologies in which energy displaces human labor, thereby intensifying unemployment. The effort to meet environmental standards has sharply increased the price of nuclear power, automobiles, and synthetic chemicals, and has diverted capital from productive investments in the steel industry. Capital, which is also in increasing demand to support the new technologies and to sustain energy production, is in short supply, seriously limiting new investment and economic growth. As a result, proponents of enhanced capital formation have already called for "reduced consumption," implying once more a lowered standard of living.

Thus, the United States has become the richest, most affluent country in human history, but the means used to reach this exalted state—particularly our reliance on production technologies based on unlimited use of resources and unrestrained impact on the environment—have created serious economic difficulties as well. The very means of our past success threaten out future.

This contradiction is now widely recognized. But there is also widespread frustration, a sense of impotence before the huge, complex task of resolving it. And even if we understood what to do, the means of doing it—political action—is itself regarded with suspicion. As Christopher Lasch has pointed out recently:

> It is no secret that Americans have lost faith in politics. . . .A growing despair of changing society—even of understanding it—has generated on the one hand a revival of old-time religion, on the other a cult of expanding consciousness, health, and personal "growth." . . . To live for the moment is the prevailing passion—to live for yourself, not for your predecessors or posterity. We are fast losing the sense of historical continuity, the sense of belonging to a succession of generations originating in the past and stretching into the future.[1]

If we are to negotiate the historic passage mandated by the conflict between our resources and our means of using them, we shall have to shake off the politics of despair and discover the links between the *nature* of the problems and our seeming inability to solve them. Otherwise despair can only become a self-fulfilling prophecy.

The recent campaign for the presidency is a particularly challenging opportunity to seek such a connection. To most of us the presidential election of 1976 was a strange and unsettling experience. The candidates campaigned hard; they traveled across the nation, fervently speaking in their own support and against the opponent; they debated face to face, defending their own positions and attacking each other's. Yet, the campaign was nearly unanimously condemned for its failure to get at the issues. In announcing its support for Mr. Carter, the *New York Times* complained that the two contestants were ". . . unable in three nationally televised debates adequately to articulate their respective philosophies of government or to clarify the political, economic and moral issues that divide them."[2] In the opposite camp, the *Wall Street Journal* began a series of editorials on the election by declaring: "Well, if the candidates aren't going to talk about the issues, somebody ought to."[3]

What was wrong? After all, Mr. Carter and Mr. Ford certainly told us where they stood on nearly every conceivable national issue: unemployment, inflation, bureaucracy and the cost of government, environmental quality, the energy problem, medical care, military expenditures, foreign relations. Surely these issues are sufficiently relevant to the nation's future to satisfy the most exacting editorial writer, and contentious enough to carry the most apathetic voter into the polls. What was missing?

What was missing were the *questions* which, after all, ought to logically precede the numerous answers that the candidates so eagerly thrust upon us. The most important—and most neglected—question is "Why?"

Consider, for example, the candidates' pronouncements on unemployment. Mr. Ford contended that the total number of employed people has actually increased, and that the economy is sound enough to create even more jobs if business is suitably stimulated by tax incentives. For his part, Mr. Carter promised to reduce unemployment from the present average rate of nearly 8 percent to 3 or 4 percent, if need be by government action.

These are answers, of a sort. But what is the *question*? What is it that troubles the nearly 40 percent of black teenagers who are unable to find work? What is on their minds, as they look for their first job, testing, for the first time, their economic worth to society—only to make the shattering discovery that there is no place for them in the national economy? The question that must concern

the unemployed, and the rest of us as we ponder their predicament, is not how to trim a few percentage points off the unemployment rate, but *why*—in the richest, most affluent society—there is
not enough work for everyone. The real question was stated quite
simply by Cardinal O'Connell of Boston in an earlier time, 1931:

> Unemployment is a ghastly failure of industrial leadership—What is
> the flaw in the capitalist system which has governed industry for a
> couple of centuries that it creates and cannot resolve this paradox?[4]

Cardinal O'Connell's question gives meaning to the often un-
expressed feeling that the separate topics of debate in the recent
campaign—the shaky economy, the energy problem, continuing
degradation of the environment, the intractable urban crisis—are
only symptoms of a much larger problem. In the words of one
citizen who was recently interviewed about "voter apathy," "The
President of the United States isn't going to solve our problems.
The problems are too big."[5] The voters were not "apathetic";
rather, they were too deeply concerned with serious questions to
be interested in trivial answers. They sensed the imminence of a
major change in the nation's course, a change in their own lives
that will drastically affect their children's. In the absence of an
understanding of the change there is a foreboding that the country's future is destined to be much worse than its recent past.

What was lacking in the recent campaign was just such a
sense of history—a framework, an analysis, which as least attempts
to explain, to link together, the multitude of seemingly insoluble
problems for which the candidates cheerfully provided their "answers." The whole problem is indeed too big for the President to
solve; but it is surely his responsibility to identify the problem, to
define it, so that society as a whole can seek to resolve it. That is
what the electorate missed in the candidates.

Historians are agreed that the elections of 1840 through
1856—those hard-to-remember presidencies of Tyler, Polk, Taylor, Fillmore, Pierce, and Buchanan—represent a low point in national politics, generating campaigns that were probably even more
frustrating than the recent one. And, again, it is instructive to ask
that much-neglected question: "Why?"

In an account of the 1856 campaign by Murat Halstead, a distinguished journalist of the time, we can find passages, strangely appropriate to the 1976 election, concerning the launching by frustrated voters of a campaign for "Nobody":

> We do not believe, if the question is reduced to this, that the people much care whether Buchanan or Fremont, or Nobody is elected to the presidency. . . . Upon the important question of the day, Messrs. Buchanan and Fremont stand upon equal grounds—they are negatives. Their nomination would emasculate the presidential campaign, and render the great and solemn trial of the highest question in our politics a farce as ridiculous as the drama of the Prince of Denmark, with the part of Hamlet omitted.[6]

That highest question was, of course, slavery.

According to the historian James Morgan, Buchanan's election marked the end of

> an ignominious era which opened with the accession of Tyler and closed with the inauguration of Lincoln. All through it, the politicans—yes, and the people too—were only preparing for the great tragedy of 1861-65. They foolishly thought they were averting it, but no one ever escaped trouble by running away from it. . . . Like the other presidents of his futile generation, Buchanan was chosen not to lead on the slavery question, but to mislead the country.[7]

What trivialized the election campaigns that preceded Lincoln's was the candidates' elaborate, often raucous efforts to divert the voter's attention from the "highest question," to *avoid* a national decision on the issue of slavery. Even Lincoln, who at last brought the country face to face with the problem, was warned by his friends when he read to them the opening statement prepared for the 1858 debates with Douglas ("A house divided against itself cannot stand. I believe that this Government cannot endure permanently half slave and half free. . . . ") that this speech would lead to defeat in the senatorial race. Despite his friends' advice to change the speech, Lincoln chose to "leave it to the world unerased."[8] He lost the election. Lincoln preferred defeat to further avoidance of the slavery issue, and in that principled defeat laid the basis for his election as President, when two years later the nation at last took the first essential step toward resolving the issue of slavery—by confronting it. That the means included the tragedy of the Civil

War ought not obscure the crucial historic fact—that the issue was at last confronted, and resolved.

What is it that we are trying to run away from today? What is the unspoken issue that reduced the recent presidential campaign to trivialities and irrelevancies?

I propose to develop the thesis that the seemingly intractable problems that have burdened the campaign with superficial answers are symptoms of a deeper, much more basic fault. I believe that this deep fault is the dimly perceived source of the popular unease, the sense that we confront a problem "too big to be solved by the President." The issues that *were* recognizable in the recent campaign—the instability of the economy; the degradation of the environment; the threat to survival generated by our very productive capabilities; the wasteful, largely futile bureaucracies created to correct these faults—are some of the symptoms of this basic fault. And it is this fault that threatens to block the historic passage which is mandated by the clash between our resources and our present means of using them.

It is the inability—and perhaps the fear—of confronting the enormous implications of this flaw which smothered the recent campaign in a wave of obfuscation, thereby resurrecting the politics of avoidance. If we are to weather the impending historic passage we must make an effort to understand it, to put an end to the politics of despair. On these grounds, we have no choice but to seek out the hidden flaw, to define it, to discuss what might be done to correct it. This essay is a contribution to that task.

How have the relationships between the nation's resources and the social values that have been achieved by using them—a high (on the average) and increasing standard of living together with continued growth of the productive system itself—so changed as to place new limits on these goals? I shall restrict the consideration of this issue to a single resource, energy, partly because of its generic importance, and also because of the relatively detailed data that are available, as compared with other resources.

We can envision the steps which lead from the acquisition of an energy source to the desired social values in the following general and highly simplified form:

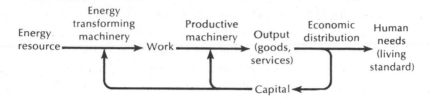

The system's ability to support the standard of living is dependent on the net efficiency of the overall process that leads from the resources to the application of the system's output to human needs. Growth represents the enlargement of the production system, and therefore depends on the availability of capital, which is, in turn, derived from the system's output. Hence the relationship between resources and the growth of production depends not only on the system's overall efficiency, but also on the specific efficiency with which capital is used to convert energy resources into productive work and to produce the productive machinery itself. Finally it should be noted that the system's output is divided *betwen* the two social goals of enhanced living standards and growth (as governed by capital). Thus, if we assume that the social purpose of the system's growth is itself to enlarge the system's abliity to meet human needs, then growth must proceed in a way that does not unduly consume capital, and so reduce the share of the output that is devoted to the overriding social purpose.

The U. S. production system relies heavily on nonrenewable energy sources, especially petroleum and natural gas. Although domestic supplies of these fuels are by no means physically exhausted as yet, the *economic* effects of their nonrenewability are already being felt. As oil, for example, is depleted and more work and capital is needed to tap deeper and more scattered deposits, the efficiency of the extraction process declines. This can be measured by the productivity of capital invested in domestic oil production. In 1974, oil representing 16.8 million BTU was produced per year

per dollar of invested capital, while the figure projected for 1988 is
expected to fall to 4.5 million BTU. According to a Federal Energy
Administration (FEA) report, an effort to *increase* domestic oil production by only 15 percent would result in a rise from the present
average price of $9.25 per barrel to a marginal price of about $39
per barrel. The law of diminishing returns is at work.[9]

A similar process affects the cost of producing natural gas and
uranium fuel. But since coal deposits are relatively large and later-
ally distributed, the effect of diminishing returns on this resource
has not been felt as yet. However, if in response to declining supplies of domestic petroleum we develop synthetic liquid fuels from
coal, the productivity of capital would fall by a factor of 10, relative
to the direct production of coal itself. Such high capital costs are
also involved in the production of shale oil.[10] Much of these high
capital costs are due to measures for controlling environmental
hazards.

Once a fuel has been produced, work must be extracted from
it by some suitable energy-transfer machine—an oil burner, gaso-
line engine, a coal-fired or nuclear power plant. Two main factors
affect the overall, or social, efficiency of this step: (a) the thermodynamic effeciency of the equipment, that is, the amount of work
actually used for a task, relative to the minimum work needed to
accomplish it; and (b) its economic efficiency, that is, the productivity of the capital that is invested in it (as measured by the amount
of work yielded per dollar of invested capital).

A study by the American Physical Society[11] provides the first
overall picture of the efficiency with which energy is used in the
U. S. production system. Carried out from the point of view of the
Second (or more relevant) Law of Thermodynamics, this study indicates that the overall efficiency is on the order of 10 to 15 percent.
A very large part of the energy used in the U. S. is used unneces-
sarily, wasted. At the same time the capital productivity of energy
transfer processes— that is, the useful work obtained per dollar of
capital investment in the energy transfer machinery—has declined.
Power plants have a particularly low capital productivity, and electricity therefore becomes the most expensive form of energy.[12] If

electricity is used in resistance heaters for space heat and hot water—tasks that can be accomplished by less valuable forms of energy—the thermodynamic efficiency is less than 1 percent. Because
30 percent of the electricity generated in the U. S is used for space
heat and hot water, a great deal of the huge capital investment in
power production is, in effect, wasted. Finally, capital efficiency has
been further decreased by the introduction of technologically im-
mature nuclear power plants, which each year demand greater
amounts of capital to install equipment needed to deal with newly
recognized safety and waste disposal problems.

The combined effect of these factors has been an overall decline in the productivity of capital in energy production, which has
fallen from 2,250,000 BTU/dollar in 1960 to 2,168,000 BTU/dollar
in 1970, to 1,845,000 BTU/dollar in 1975. This means that an increasing share of the wealth which could have been available to
meet human needs has been diverted, instead, toward building the
productive machinery that is justified by being devoted to this
task.[13]

In 1973 all of these processes converged to create an unprecedented economic situation. The *Organization of Petroleum Export-
ing Countries* (OPEC) imposed an oil embargo and increased the
price of oil. But these dramatic events only triggered changes
which would have happened in any case, because of diminishing
returns in the production of domestic oil and natural gas, and because of the effort to introduce expensive energy technologies such
as nuclear power and synthetic fuels. Although for more than
twenty years before 1973 the price of energy in the U. S., relative
to the price of commodities in general, had remained essentially
constant, the relative energy price since 1973 has increased sharply,
and continues to soar.[14] This situation is unprecedented in the history of the U. S.; at no other time since 1811 (when government
statistics were established) has there been such a rapid, sustained
increase in the relative price of energy. It has already resulted in a
sharp increase in the rate of general inflation (the annual percent
increase in wholesale price index, which averaged 3 percent per
year between 1965 and 1973, rose to 13 percent in 1973 and 18
percent in 1974).[15] The rise in energy price also threatens to reduce

the economic value of investments in particularly energy-intensive industries (or for that matter in "all-electric" homes, which will decline in value as electricity, the most expensive form of energy, rises in price). In these ways the recent changes in the energy sector have begun directly to erode the standard of living.

If we turn to the next step in the overall production system—the conversion of work (and other) imputs into the output of goods—a trend toward inefficiency is again evident. In the last twenty-five to thirty years, industrial processes with relatively high energy and capital productivities have been rapidly displaced by sectors with much lower ones. Classical examples are the displacement of natural materials, such as leather, by synthetic substitutes, such as plastics. The production of plastics in the period 1948–70 increased at an average annual rate of about 16 percent per year, while leather production increased an average of about one percent per year.[16] As plastic goods have replaced leather ones (and synthetic fibers, detergents and plastics have displaced natural fibers, soap and wood), the efficiency with which energy resources and the wealth embodied in industrial capital are used to produce textiles, cleansers and furniture has declined. In the last few years, a similar process has begun to affect the white-collar sectors. As automation has been introduced into printing, financial operations and communication, they too have become increasingly dependent on energy and capital.

A similar pattern emerges from the sweeping changes in U. S. agriculture in the last twenty-five to thirty years. In that period the resource base of agriculture has shifted dramatically toward industrial, energy-intensive inputs, especially of chemicals such as fertilizers and pesticides. These changes have tied agriculture to the economic behavior of the petrochemical industry, which produces not only tractor fuels but the propane used for grain-drying, the ammonia used in nitrogen fertilizer, as well as pesticides and other farm chemicals. In the last few years, the sharply rising cost of energy has been reflected in two- and three fold increases in the price of fertilizers and pesticides.[17] This has linked farm prices to the economic effects of diminishing returns in the fuel sector, contributing to the inflation of food prices and to the erosion of living standards, especially among the poor. A similar process has been underway in transportation. Since 1945 automobile, truck, and air-line traffic has been substituted for railroad traffic, with consider-able overall reduction in the productivity of energy (i.e., passen-ger- or ton-miles per BTU) and of capital (i.e., passenger- or ton-miles per invested dollar).[18] The cost of getting to and from work has risen sharply, again depressing living standards.

When these changes are added to the corresponding reduc-tions in energy and capital productivity in the energy-conversion steps, it becomes evident that the overall efficiency with which energy is applied to human needs has suffered a considerable re-duction in the last thirty years. Although the output of the produc-tion system has grown, the capital and energy needed to sustain it have grown faster.[19] As a result, both energy and capital are in short supply. The energy shortage is now met by imports. The capital shortage—the subject of recent concern in the business community—threatens serious economic dislocations: demands for reduced corporate taxes, for reduced consumption, and for redis-tribution of wealth in favor of the rich—steps designed to increase savings and thus aid the formation of investment capital.[20]

It remains to be said that while energy and capital productiv-ities have decreased, there has been a general *increase* in the pro-ductivity of labor, which in manufacturing industries has tripled in the past thirty years. Most of the displacements cited earlier, such as the displacement of natural by synthetic materials, involve a very marked increase in labor productivity. Thus, in the produc-tion of leather, labor productivity amounts to $6.25 of value added per man-hour (in 1971), much less than the figure of $27.75 for the manufacture of chemicals and allied products, including plastics.[21] This is a modern example of the process, first elucidated in Marx's analysis of classical capitalism, in which capital displaces labor. These intensified demands for energy resources that are nonre-newable and inefficient in their use of capital have contributed to the sharply escalating price of energy and the heavy demand for capital.

This brief account shows, I believe, that the ways in which energy is produced and used in the production system are deeply faulted. We have fostered the unnecessary use of capital-intensive energy equipment, such as electric power stations. In agriculture, manufacturing, and transportation we have encouraged production processes that are particularly wasteful of energy and capital, and hazardous to the environment, displacing processes which were more thrifty and benign. These changes have worsened an array of serious economic difficulties, including unemployment, inflation, and the shortage of capital. In sum, because the postwar growth of the U. S. system of production has depended heavily on the introduction of increasingly energy- and capital-intensive production technologies, it has itself generated countervailing economic forces. These have begun to limit both the system's rate of growth and its ability to meet human needs.

How can we explain this failure? What has failed is not the gross productive capacity of the system, for clearly that continues to grow. The failure is in the nature of what the system produces, in its *pattern* of growth. Wealth has been invested in new production which is inefficient in its use of energy, of capital, and of the environment—and inadequate in its ability to generate employment. The locus of the fault must lie, therefore, in the system's *governance*—the pattern of decisions that determines how its wealth is invested, and for what purpose.

It is useful, here, to recall a general observation that I have made earlier (in *The Poverty of Power*) regarding the relationships that govern the interactions among the ecosystem, the production system and the economic system: Economic considerations, in particular the hoped-for rate of return, determine the design of productive enterprises, which in turn impose their effects—that are so frequently harmful—on the ecosystem. Economists have told us a great deal about the economic process that is supposed to govern the productive uses of wealth—in Heilbroner's term, "The ubiquitous market network, where both factors of production and goods and services are bought and sold." The basic mechanism is exchange: Two parties undertake voluntarily to exchange goods or services in the expectation (or hope) of mutual benefit. The kinds of goods and the method of production are governed by the expectation that the ultimate exchange will be beneficial to the producer in yielding a profit, and to the buyer in satisfying his needs. There are two noteworthy processes that characterize this method of exchange, and at the same time help to explain our current predicament. First, since the production and selling of goods on the market are governed only by the producer's profit and the buyer's satisfaction, this process is a *private* one, impervious to the interests of the society that must bear any harmful consequences. Second, this process need only reflect the short time span required to satisfy the personal interests of the exchange, while the long-term consequences of the exchange are again borne by society.

If we turn now to the list of current problems—unemployment, inflation, bureaucracy, environmental degradation, urban decay—which were so avidly "answered" by the candidates in the recent election campaign, we discover a common feature: All of these are concerns that are *not* taken into account in the conventional market exchange mechanism. In the parlance of conventional economics they are all "externalities." These factors have no role in the voluntary, mutually beneficial, private process of exchange because they are involuntary in their origin, harmful in their effects, and social rather than private in their impact. All these issues affect the individual not through an exchange relationship with another individual partner, but through society as a whole. Thus, the basic mechanism that governs the operation of the U. S. economic system excludes from consideration precisely those *social* effects that were the subject of the recent election debates. This creates a sharp imbalance in the relationship between the governance of production decisions and the rest of society. Although these decisions have a heavy, often deleterious effect on society, social interests have no *direct* way of participating in them.

In terms of our initial concern, all this is to make the relatively simple point that although the avowed purposed of the U. S. economic system—to meet its people's needs—is social, social purpose is excluded from its governance. This is to say, of course, that the U. S. economy is almost entirely governed by private decisions, made by those who own and control the capital needed to establish a production enterprise; it is, after all, a private enterprise, capitalist system.

Of course, the social needs have not been totally ignored. Especially since the New Deal, social institutions have been created to ameliorate the various social ills, the lamentable externalities that have emanated from our otherwise successful economic system. But these institutions have not *solved* the problems they were created to deal with. The numerous welfare agencies have not, after all, eliminated unemployment, poverty, and inadequate medical care. Indeed, these remedial efforts have now themselves become a problem—the onerous ecomonic and political burden of a growing bureaucracy. Again it is useful to ask, *Why?*

The reason the bureaucratic efforts to deal with unemployment, inflation, the energy problem and environmental degradation seem so often to fail—and in their failure even further expand—is that they intervene at a point far removed from the site at which the damage is done. Consider the unemployment problem. For reasons already discussed, nearly half of the U. S. unemployment problem is due to the continued reduction in the number of workers needed to produce a unit of output, that is, the vaunted rise in labor productivity. Thus the problem originates at that point where a decision is made to introduce new production machinery or processes that reduce labor input. But the remedial action takes place only long after the problem has been created, and people are, in fact, already unemployed. *Then*, society intervenes. The unemployed person is directed into an elaborate and expensive bureaucracy: interviews are conducted; forms are filled out; computer cards are punched; data are processed; until finally the person receives an unemployment check and the social goal—that even if unemployed no one should starve or otherwise suffer serious deprivation—is achieved. How much simpler it would be if there were, in fact, a job available. But this would require that the social signal represented by rising unemployment should be fed back into the system so as to stimulate the creation of jobs at the point where that decision is made—the design of the means of production. Like the present system of unemployment insurance, this process would also involve social intervention. But now the intervention would be designed to remedy the fault at its *source* rather than merely attempting to remedy its effects by adding a costly and burdensome bureaucracy. If social governance were exerted at the point where the problem is created—at the decision-making point in the production system—unemployment would become, in effect, a self-correcting problem that would lessen with time. Under the present arrangements, social intervention is exerted in such a way that it has no effect on the causes of unemployment, but can only ameliorate the symptoms. As long as the governance of the production system remains largely impervious to a meaningful, operational social response, unemployment will continue unabated and the resultant bureaucracy will continue to proliferate.

The same situation exists in connection with environmental degradation. It is now clear that the locus of the cause of pollution is in the design of the means of production: smog is the inevitable outcome of the postwar shift to high compression auto engines; radiation hazards derive from the introduction of nuclear technology into the production of electricity and weapons; chemical disasters, such as Kepone in Virginia, PBB in Michigan, dioxin in Italy, are a result of the huge growth of the petrochemical industry, which displaces natural products. But we have ignored these origins of pollution and have only attempted to correct the symptoms: Exhaust devices are mandated for autos; nuclear power plants are enveloped in expensive controls and regulations; chemical products are subjected to elaborate new tests. As a result huge new bureaucracies— EPA, OSHA, FEA, FDA[22]—are now involved in the hopeless and expensive process of patching up environmental damage, after it has occurred, when much of the damage may be irreversible, and all of it costly.

Often enough the impact of production technologies is so great that after-the-fact remedies are indeed impossible. For example, as a result of the decision taken more than thirty years ago to produce PCBs for a variety of industrial uses, these highly toxic materials have been irreversibly disseminated into the environment, with effects that no one can foresee or control. Only now have manufacturers been persuaded to abandon PCB production.

How much better it would have been if this decision had been made thirty years ago, when it was discovered that nearly all of the workers in the first PCB plant were suffering from serious systemic poisoning. If the workers could have participated in the managerial decision to produce a substance as toxic as PCB in the first place, production might have ended long ago; we could have avoided the huge assault of PCB on the environment. If the public concern with environmental pollution could influence the problem at its point of origin, we could have been spared the huge bureaucratic burden of later attempting to minimize it.

It could be argued, perhaps, that it was once possible to ignore concerns such as dwindling resources, environmental degradation, or even some low rate of unemployment, since after all, living standards *were* rising and production steadily increasing. Now, however, it is clear that we can no longer afford the luxury of such "benign neglect." In the absence of social intervention to correct the faults in the production system that have given rise to these concerns, the faults themselves now impede the very goals that the system is supposed to serve. We can no longer avoid the task of learning how to introduce social governance into the decisions that determine the design of the means of production—what kinds of energy sources and productive machines are used, what kinds of goods are produced. If we fail to meet this new imperative, problems of resource depletion, environmental degradation, unemployment and capital shortage will persist and efforts to ameliorate—rather than solve—them will only add to our burdens the final insult of a growing bureaucracy.

In sum, I believe that if we are to solve the knot of intractable problems that seem to be "too big for the President" the nation must now confront a basic, overriding issue. This issue is how to establish, consistent with the nation's unshakable devotion to political freedom, forms of governance over the U. S. system of production that will enable these social concerns, themselves, to govern how the system operates, and thus establish in the system a self-correcting means of dealing with its own faults.

Here we can begin to perceive the hidden, unspoken issue that trivialized the recent campaign. Like the earlier social intervention into the U. S. production system—the abolition of slavery—this unspoken issue raises very grave moral and political questions. And like the slavery issue in its time, many people may prefer to avoid this new, equally disturbing one. It is therefore not surprising that—like those who gave advice to Lincoln in his debates with Douglas—the candidates in the recent election felt compelled, in the interest of winning, to avoid so contentious and alienating an issue. And inevitably, like Fremont and Buchanan before them, the candidates found themselves talking not about the deep, troublesome issues—their common roots in the transformed system of production—but about symptoms and picayune trivialities. The airwaves and newspapers were filled with a multitude of answers, while the voters waited in vain for the candidates to give voice to a single question—about unemployment, inflation, and all the other intractable crises—*Why?*

But the history of the slavery question teaches us another important lesson. When the question was at last confronted, and the people of the United States intervened in the system of production to put an end to its access to slave labor, enormous new gains in production became possible. As long as slavery persisted the nation could not take full advantage of the industrial revolution. As long as slave labor was readily available, the South remained tied to a purely agricultural, stagnant economy. And, as long as such a major section of the U. S. economy lagged behind, the modernization of U. S. production technology as a whole could not advance. Difficult as it was and although tragically bloodied by the Civil War, the decision to end slavery—to enforce that much social governance over the means of production—was necessary before the country could embark upon the huge industrial and agricultural expansion that followed.

What we now confront is the consequence of the *partial* nature of the intervention that took place more than a century ago. Although the right of society to intervene on the specific issue of slavery was accepted, this did not establish the more general principle that production itself is a social process which must be governed by social interest. The results of that failure are now upon us. Once again, the productive powers of the nation falter and the economy rapidly drifts into crisis because we have thus far failed to confront the new imperative for social governance. It takes little insight to become aware of the strange paradox facing the U. S. economy: on the one hand, growing unemployment and under-used productive capacity, and on the other the pressing need to create the new enterprises that are mandated by the imperative to spare energy and other resources and to care for the quality of the environment: electrified railroads, especially for mass transit; ur-ban electric trolley systems; solar energy systems, immediately for heating, and soon after for power; new, decentralizied production facilities that alleviate the wasteful use of energy in transportation, and the plague of throwaway containers; industrial production based more on natural materials (cotton, wool, fat, wood) than on synthetics that waste nonrenewable fuels and spread toxins into the environment; the restoration of organic matter to agriculture, which could then sustain food production instead of burdening the environment with waste.

There are a variety of known techniques, and probably a good number yet to be invented, which offer alternative ways of intro-ducing social governance into production: national planning; local or regional planning; tax and other incentives that favor proper resource and environmental decisions; and, indeed, public owner-ship on a national or local level. But these can only become alterna-tives when they are set within a framework in which the guiding principle that governs the production system is social rather than private, so that the system is designed to maximize social value.

Obviously such a goal would clash with the present form of governance, which in almost every case has as its goal the maximi-zation of private profit. It has been argued that private profit is the best motive for efficient production; but this claim is now consider-ably weakened by the common tendency, in production, toward the inefficient use of resources and capital. It will also be argued that "social governance," while a fine-sounding phrase in the ab-stract, when put into practice—for example in the Soviet Union and other socialist countries—inevitably creates political con-straints that are inimical to our own commitment to civil liberties and to democratic government. This is a legitimate concern, but it is based on the fear that the United States will be unable to bring to bear on this issue the political resources which have in the past enabled us to protect our liberties from erosion or assault. We have, after all, in only the last two decades thrown back the attack on civil liberties typified by McCarthyism and have forced Mr. Nixon to beat an ignominious retreat from his powerful attempt to subvert the democratic governance of the nation.

Recognition that the further intrusion of social interests in the system of production does, indeed, run the risk of political oppression is essential. And skepticism that we can discover how to combine the economic democracy of socialism with a humanistic concern for personal freedom and a firm commitment to democratic government may be justified. But there is, I believe, nothing to be gained by allowing the fear of failing in this goal to foreclose an effort to achieve it.

If, instead, we confront these issues in the confidence that we can resolve them, we can, I am convinced master the new historic passage and at last fully devote the nation's resources to the welfare of its people.

Notes

1. Christopher Lasch, "The Narcissist Society," *The New York Review of Books*, September 30, 1976, p. 5.
2. *New York Times*, October 24, 1976.
3. *Wall Street Journal*, October 27, 1976.
4. Arthur Schlesinger, *The Age of Roosevelt: The Crisis of the Old Order, 1919–1933* (Boston: Houghton Mifflin, 1957), p. 181.
5. *New York Times*, October 26, 1976.
6. William B. Hesseltine and Rex G. Fisher, eds., *Trimmers, Trucklers, and Temporizers: Notes of Murat Halstead from the Political Conventions of 1856* (Madison: The State Historical Society of Wisconsin, 1969), p.80.
7. James Morgan, *Our Presidents*, 3d ed. (Toronto: Macmillan, 1969), p. 127.

8. *Ibid.*, p. 140.

9. Barry Commoner, *The Poverty of Power* (New York: Knopf, 1976), p. 59.

10. Barry Commoner, testimony in U. S. Senate, Committee on Interior and Insular Affairs, Subcommittee on Energy Research and Water Resources, *Hearings on the Energy Research and Development Administration's National Energy Plan*, 94th Cong., 2d sess., July 29, 1976 (Washington, D. C.: Government Printing Office, 1976), Table I.

11. K. W. Ford et al., eds., *Efficient Use of Energy*, American Physical Society Studies on the Technical Aspects of the More Efficient Use of Energy (New York: American Institute of Physics, 1975), pp. 4, 32, 35; and for a discussion of various thermodynamic efficiencies, see Commoner, *The Poverty of Power*, pp. 38–39.

12. Commoner, testimony in *Hearings on Energy Plan*, Table I.

13. See Commoner, *The Poverty of Power*, note for p. 214.

14. See Commoner, testimony in *Hearings on Energy Plan*, Figure 2.

15. U. S. Bureau of the Census, *Statistical Abstract of the United States* (Washington, D. C.: Government Printing Office, 1975), Figure 14–1.

16. See Commoner, *The Poverty of Power*, p. 200.

17. *Ibid.*, p. 167.

18. *Ibid.*, pp. 179–90.

19. This is true of the production of goods. Service industries, which have been less energy- and capital-intensive than manufacturing, have grown relatively faster, tending to compensate for the changes in the manufacturing sectors. Now, however, automation in the service industries has begun to increase their energy- and capital intensiveness.

20. *Ibid.*, p. 302.

21. *Ibid.*, p. 201.

22. Respectively, Environmental Protection Agency, Occupational Safety and Health Administration, Federal Energy Administration, and Food and Drug Administration.

GUNNAR MYRDAL

5.

RACE AND CLASS IN A WELFARE STATE

TOWARD THE END of the 1930s and the beginning of the 1940s I labored with a rather intensive and comprehensive study of what was then called the "Negro problem." This work compelled me to try to make explicit the value premises steering fact finding and analysis. Things look different depending upon "where you stand." Prior to answers there must be questions. And there can be no view except from a viewpoint. In the questions raised and the viewpoint applied valuations are implied. In *An American Dilemma* the set of value premises selected, made explicit and tested for relevance, significance, consistency and feasibility I called the "American Creed." But I could just as well have called it "National Purpose."

The national purpose represents a moral commitment of the American nation to certain high ideals. These ideals of the essential dignity of the individual human being, of the fundamental equality of all men, and of certain inalienable rights to liberty, justice, and fair opportunity represent to the American people the essential

73

meaning of the nation's early struggle for independence. Rooted in the Enlightenment philosophy of Natural Law, in Christianity, and in the English common law, these ideals were pressed into the nation's constitutional documents and elaborated upon by all national leaders, thinkers, and statesmen. Hammered upon continuously in the attempt to consolidate a nation composed of people having such diverse origins, the ideals which comprised the national purpose became highly conscious to all Americans, including, as I then could observe, the oppressors as well as the oppressed. In spite of all the conspicuous and systematic gross failures of compliance, America, of all the countries I knew, had come to have the most explicitly formulated system of general ideals in reference to human interrelations, shared, on one level of valuations, by all its citizens.

Specifying this system of ideals for different spheres of life, I found them, as ideals, on the whole clear-cut and unambiguous, for instance in regard to justice and civic rights. The one exception was the ambiguity concerning the meaning of economic equality and its relation to liberty—an ambiguity which could be found at the beginning of the nation's existence and still persists today. But in so far as black people's poverty was seen to be caused by discrimination in the labor market or elsewhere, the national purpose became challenged in one of its most specific precepts: equal opportunities.

From the beginning of the new nation, however, the great majority of the then about 20 percent of Americans who were black were held in slavery. In the context of the national purpose this constituted an American dilemma, which, remained even after slavery was abolished. It has not yet been resolved, though there have been epochs of sweeping changes, sometimes toward deterioration but in the longer view mainly toward an improvement in the status of blacks.

That the elevated ideals of the national purpose were not the only, or even the dominant, valuations was obvious thirty-five years ago as to a large extent it is today. In the South, where then more than three-fourths of the blacks were living, an institutional and later even a legal structure had been built up after Reconstruction to keep them suppressed. A whole ideology blatantly contradicting the national purpose had taken shape and was upheld by an almost "Solid South." In the North, without a legal framework to enforce color-caste there was nevertheless much institutionalized segregation and discrimination.

The main point stressed in *An American Dilemma* was that within an individual soul or in a group of people there is not just one logically homogeneous set of valuations but usually a mesh of struggling inclinations, interests, and ideals. The valuations on the higher level are always to some extent suppressed, with the conflict hidden from full consciousness by means of opportunistically distorted beliefs about reality. There are in fact no solid "attitudes," a concept to which I am therefore allergic. When recorded, "attitudes" regularly show up to be ambiguous in content and unstable in time. And more particularly they conceal valuational dilemmas. From one point of view human behavior is regularly a moral compromise.

But even when the valuations on the higher level, where the ideals of the national purpose are located, are blunted and overlaid by all sorts of contrary beliefs and valuations they do have their reality and are never entirely without influence. They might even, in the longer historical perspective, determine the trend of development, as thirty-five years ago I found reasons to believe and as I believe even more firmly today.

The persistent reality of the national purpose in a society that systematically breaks its prescripts implies that, with varying strength, the national purpose becomes itself a social force among many others. Inscribed in the constitutional documents, the ideals of the national purpose are applied more or less fully by the Supreme Court with ramifications extending to the other federal courts and often far beyond. The intensity of this intrusion of the national purpose into the life of the nation has changed over the two centuries. There has always been a question of how far the authorities mentioned dare to go against the prejudices of the people and, of course, of how prejudiced the persons holding this judicial prerogative are themselves—prejudices being understood as valuations and beliefs contradicting the national purpose.

Fundamentally, the force of the national purpose depends, of course, on how firmly it is based in the heart of the American nation, which at any time could change the Constitution away from expressing these ideals. At no time has any such radical negation of the national purpose been seriously proposed.

At the end of the 1930s and the beginning of the 1940s the status of black people in the South had remained fairly stagnant for more than half a century—since the national compromise of the 1870s when, after Reconstruction, they were delivered back to the embittered Southern whites with no means of defending themselves. From intensive analysis of what was on the way to happening in the South, the conclusion was drawn in *An American Dilemma* that this long era of nearly complete stagnation in race relations was coming to an end. It was even asserted that "not since Reconstruction had there been more reason to anticipate fundamental changes in American race relations, changes that will involve a development toward American ideals." The Black Revolt was foreseen and also that it would have its beginning in the South: "America can never more regard its Negroes as a patient, submissive minority. Negroes will continuously become less well 'accommodated.' They will organize for defense and offense." That the blacks in their struggle could, and would, appeal to the ideals of the national purpose was certain.

With American participation in World War II, the United States had to stand before the whole world as a defender of racial tolerance and racial equality against the Nazis. The fact that the Japanese in their propaganda utilized anti-white feelings in Asia made it even more imperative to stress the racial equality doctrine. The national purpose and its ideals—liberty, justice, and equality of opportunity without regard to race, creed or color—were now ringing out in fullness. With this renewed activation of the national purpose followed generally in the North confessions of the serious shortcomings in regard to observance at home of these ideals and a renewed commitment to reform. Even in the South, for a short time, the liberals became more courageous and outspoken. That all this fostered cynical mistrust and increased the angry bitterness among blacks in the South was easily observable.

Among the nonliberal white Southerners, the smug and opportunistic complacency that they remained the unchallenged masters of the situation in the region was being undermined. Behind this change was not only a new awareness of black dissatisfaction with their caste role but also fear that the North would renew and intensify its efforts to reform them against their will.

When in the autumn of 1942 I wrote the last chapter of *An American Dilemma*, I foresaw a confrontation. I could record that even some black leaders, and not only the most accommodating ones, were apprehensive about the future. But it would take some thirteen years before the Black Revolt broke out.

Meanwhile, all the incipient changes in the conditions of life and work of blacks in the South that I had recorded continued, many of them with increasing speed. President Harry S. Truman attempted to get the federal government active in order to secure more civil rights for blacks. The Supreme Court's decisions went steadily and more definitely toward a closer confromity with the national purpose by increasingly protecting the blacks' rights to equality. The unanimous decision in the *Brown* case in 1954, which ordered the desegregation of schools, implied a culmination.

With few exceptions the whites in the South remained, however, in fierce opposition to attempts to change race relations in their region. After the *Brown* decision, for instance, there was massive resistance and for many years they used all available means to hinder more than token compliance, if even that. To keep the blacks in their place much violence was tolerated, if not condoned, and economic reprisal was more effectively organized by the White Citizens Councils spreading over the whole South. The entire Jim Crow structure and all the enforced humiliating and disabling behavior patterns associated with it remained in full force.

Then suddenly there was a mass revolt of the blacks in the South. It began with the 1955–56 bus boycott in Montgomery. It ended after a Supreme Court decision in November 1956 declaring segregation in buses unconstitutional not only in interstate transport, as had already been ordered, but also locally.

Unlike the *Brown* decision in 1954, this decision was not an

initial spark of a change that then was slowly becoming imple-
mented; rather it served as a confirmation of the complete victory
of a successful black mass revolt. The importance of this Supreme
Court decision was that it told the white South that the law of the
land was definitely against it, and that from now on its laboriously
constructed Jim Crow state legislation would become outlawed
whenever it was challenged.

The Montgomery bus boycott had already triggered a chain
reaction of similar boycotts in other Southern cities. Within a short
time segregation on the buses had been brought to an end in practically every city. The protest movement rapidly broadened its
front: *against* the whole Jim Crow structure and discrimination at
lunch counters, stores and in the labor market and *for* organizing
blacks to register for elections and to demand more effective desegregation of schools. Within a few years race relations in the South
had been brought to undergo a fundamental change.

Montgomery, where the whole thing started, was not very
different from other Southern cities. According to Martin Luther
King's own testimony its black community suffered from "divided
leadership, indifference and complacency." He confessed that he
had almost become "persuaded that no reform could ever be
achieved in Montgomery."

A petty incident* of which there must have been thousands in
the South before and which could hardly have been more than a
precipitating event, galvanized the black community into a united
struggle that gradually widened its demands for equal rights and
spread over the whole region. King's own explanation, which I
believe is correct, was that the situation had become ripe by the

*Editor's note: On December 1, 1955, Mrs. Rosa Parks refused to vacate her bus
seat in order to comply with the white preference seating practices of the Montgomery Bus Line, a private company franchised by the city of Montgomery, Alabama.
Mrs. Parks was arrested for violation of the bus-segregation ordinance and a
one-day bus boycott was organized to coincide with her trial. Mrs. Parks was con-
victed and fined. Black leaders formed the Montgomery Improvement Association,
which organized the 99 percent effective, continuing bus boycott. A suit filed in
federal court led to the Supreme Court's decision on Novermber 13, 1956, that
segregation on the city's buses was unconstitutional and on December 21, 1956 the
bus boycott was ended.

"culmination of a slowly developing process . . . there comes a time when people get tired of being trampled by aggression."

Almost as an explosion, all the factionalism and defeatism among the black community leaders and the passivity among them and the masses disappeared. All stood together. The white establishment used all the customary devices for intimidating the blacks, including arrests, bombings, and still more threats of violence. But the entire black community stood united and firm. Decisions were taken unanimously in mass meetings in the churches, where blacks of all classes participated. Even later—when, in the continuation of the movement in various localities and with variagated purposes over the whole South most often only a small number of people actually participated in demonstrations, especially the sit-ins—the character of a mass movement was retained by the fact that entire black communities stood behind those who acted.

The remarkable thing was that this organized mass movement remained disciplined and rationally directed upon broad but attainable goals. Another part of the explanation of this movement's success was that giving up Jim Crow and other forms of blatant discrimination was, in fact, not financially expensive to the white Southerners: that whole structure was instrinsically uneconomical.

A third explanation was the strict adherence to the principle of nonviolence. The movement was prepared to use to the utmost the well-established American rights to demonstrate peacefully, to picket and to boycott, and did not shrink from disobeying unjust laws and regulations. In doing this they were prepared to sustain violence and to abstain from hitting back. This was clearly not timidity. It proved an astute political tactic. What violence occurred, and there was much of it, was committed by whites. The ordinary white American, and not only in the North, who saw splashed over the newspapers or on the television screen such images as that of police dogs attacking little black kids in Birmingham in 1963 was moved to exclaim, This is not right!

A fourth explanation is that the movement from the outset and continuously was firmly directed toward integration, to follow realization of the equal opportunities promised in the national purpose. The insistence that the movement should as far as possible be interracial was, moreover, a reasoned principle. Stress was increasingly laid upon the fact that there were also whites who were poor and exploited. For the future it was held that when blacks would get the vote they should bring whites into cooperation and coalition. It is astonishing how widely that way of thinking became accepted among the blacks in the South, and how it has remained the practical policy line both in propaganda and black politics there.

The first and astonishingly successful phase of the Black Revolt had its culmination in the March on Washington in August 1963 by more than 200,000 people, of whom almost a third were white.

The reaction to this development on the part of the American government and Congress was the civil rights bills enacted in 1964 and 1965. They were more sweepingly radical than anybody could have thought possible only a few years earlier. To me an intensely and crucially important question, on which little research has been done, is this: Why and how were the whites in the United States brought to the point where some would press for and others would accept these bills?

I do not believe they acted out of fear. The Southern Black Revolt did not imply serious danger for anybody other than those who were themselves part of the movement. Neither was the Black Revolt really much of a threat to the American power structure. Rather, it was a challenge to the consciences of the whites who held all the power.

The civil rights laws represent a major example of the ideals of the national purpose being activated as a social and political force. All people are, in the compromises of life, pleading to their consciences. In America part of people's consciences has become stamped in the mold of the national purpose, which, when circumstances so demand, can become an active social force.

These ideals stand, first as a rather firm inhibition against taking new legislative action intentionally aimed at repressing the blacks. America can be seen to live on with considerable segregation and discrimination against blacks and occasionally even experience an intensification of these behavior patterns. But it is not able to condone and legislate an open and systematic apartheid as in South Africa. It is true that in the South the ideals of the national purpose had not prevented the states from building up Jim Crow legislation. But when these laws—formulated upon the fiction of equality as a token recognition of the national purpose but clearly aimed at keeping the blacks in their lowly place—were challenged as unfair by a united, uncompromising black community, the ideals could be vitalized and the national purpose then became a dynamic force for social change.

The effectiveness of the implementation of the civil rights acts of 1964 and 1965, as also of the Supreme Court's decisions ordering desegregation of schools, has fluctuated, depending on the political climate. Nevertheless, a new direction had been given to the whole social process. After the successful Black Revolt race relations will never be the same again in the South. Jim Crow is definitely broken. The blacks are increasingly registering, voting, and entering into coalitions with whites, while watching over their own group interests. The number of black officeholders has been rising. Schools are increasingly being desegregated. Despite the many imperfections, the trend goes nevertheless in the right direction.

The Black Revolt in the South was not followed by a similar movement in the North. For almost a decade it served instead the purpose of providing volunteering black—and many white—activists in the North with a sort of vicarious theater of war, where they could live out their protest against the inequalities inflicted upon blacks in the United States.

Why during these ten years was there no movement in the North similar to the Black Revolt in the South? In this brief paper I can merely touch upon only a few of the systematic differences between the two regions. These are selected from the point of view of their importance for the blacks' reaction in the North after the successful Black Revolt in the South.

In the Southern situation there were closer bonds between the different classes of blacks. The black businessmen and professionals could monopolize black customers of all classes and had few customers outside the black community. In the North the less firm caste segregation often permitted higher class blacks to take more distance from the masses of blacks, but at the same time opened up possibilities of suspicions by the latter. In the North the potential for unity of action by the black community was thus less than in the South.

Another major difference relates to the role of the black churches. In the South they could be brought to coopereate effectively in the Black Revolt. They contributed in a major way to consolidating entire black communities into a movement holding together blacks of all classes. In particular, they were responsible for giving this movement discipline, and especially a strict adherence to the principle of nonviolence. The fact that the movement for nonviolent action was led by pastors of the churches and other church leaders must be accounted for as a main cause of general compliance with the principle.

In the big cities of the North there was greater spread of secular tendencies, and not only in the upper and middle classes. The churches there offered no similar basis for a unified protest movement. Moreover, usually, not even those black leaders in the North who endorsed the principle of nonviolent direct action or who, at least, saw clearly that violent uprisings were suicidal had much sympathy for King's message that the oppressed blacks should love, and pray for, their oppressors.

A major and systematic difference between the two regions was that in the North the blacks had, and for a long time had had, all the formal rights denied them in the South. There were no Jim Crow statutes. The school system was, in principle, flung open to them without formal rules on segregation. Public parks, playgrounds, libraries and, with exceptions, beaches and swimming pools were accessible to blacks as well as whites. Relief and social services generally were, from the time of the New Deal, made available to blacks on equal terms. In some Northern states there had even been beginnings of what was later to be called civil rights legislation against discrimination in the use of public facilities and in regard to some other matters. And in the North the blacks could register and vote.

Because the blacks in the North had for a long time had the franchise, there were black politicians. But from the ward heelers upwards they were involved in ordinary party politics, which in the big cities mostly was of the type in America called "machine politics." This implied among other things that votes were not being fully exercised in the interests of the black community. There was much cynical mistrust in the black community of those blacks engaged in the political process.

In the North the blacks had not, as in the South, been kept immobilized by threats and pressures or, with few and minor exceptions, been prevented from engaging in protest actions. Such action had instead been frequent in the North and had already a long tradition. Protests there, however, had regularly been limited to specific complaints and particular locales, for instance, against discrimination in employment in a particular business establishment or exclusion from a trade union. The closest resemblance in the North to a mass mobilization of blacks such as that of the Montgomery bus boycott was the successful threat in 1941 by A. Philip Randolph to stage a march on Washington against discrimination in the defense industry and in government employment.

Despite widespread segregation in many fields of life, segregation had not been laid down as official state policy in the North. Although there was also much discrimination, it was not formalized and was not official policy. Behind segregation and discrimination there was much race prejudice but it was less thought through than in the South and had not hardened into a caste doctrine, functioning as the openly proclaimed basis of state policy. There was no minutely prescribed racial etiquette, less emotion about social equality, no established white solidarity for the purpose of keeping blacks in their place.

While what thirty-five years ago was called the Negro problem completely dominated the politics of the South, this was definitely not so in the North. There it tended to mix and partly disappear among all other policy problems in the big cities where the blacks conglomerated. Outside those cities, the problem was still less prominent. Blacks had simply been kept from coming in.

In a sense it was more difficult for the blacks in the North to join forces and come out as a united community in direct action pressing for reform. Already having the formal rights to equality meant that blacks in the North did not have the clear and easily conceptualized targets for revolt, the very ostentatiously visible barriers to racial equality that prevailed in the South and which could unite a whole black community in revolt.

What blacks in the North faced instead was a social "system" hurting the black masses very severely by permitting segregation and discrimination on a large scale: in housing, in schooling, in the availability of employment, and so on. To organize the black community in the North to fight such a hidden system would have to be a formidable task.

That system of segregation and discrimination in the North is in a sense "private," as it is not established on the basis of public policy and law but is, on the contrary, often in blatant disobedience of law and, still more, of the declared intentions of law. It consists of millions of personal acts, or abstentions from acts, by whites and is upheld by mostly hidden, institutionalized traditions, supported by behavior inclinations of those whites directly involved. This system operates in practically all markets and, indeed, in all human relations.

It is characteristic of this social system that ordinarily a white person, even when he is directly involved, can often be unaware of the severe social and economic repercussions of what he and others are doing to the blacks. And most whites in the North are not themselves in much direct contact with the situations where blacks are maltreated. While the whites in the South were intensely conscious of their purpose, keeping the blacks down, and had gone to great lengths in openly institutionalizing and even legislating segregation and discrimination, the ordinary white in the North could easily succeed in living in innocent ignorance of the significance of what he himself was doing to the blacks, or permitting others to do. That such ignorance was convenient for his conscience served only to strengthen it.

The term often used to characterize this social system is "racism." Many whites in the North, perhaps most of them can live on without knowing a great deal about the injustices inflicted upon the blacks, feeling that in any case they themselves are absolutely innocent of racism. They can in their public opinions stand up for full equality and even vote for legislation upholding that equality. Though it certainly served the interests of whites in feeling themselves free from racism, such legislation had been less than effective in breaking the system.

To overcome the social system of racism it would be necessary forcefully to break up deeply rooted and, in their effects, broad and pervasive institutionalized conditions and behavior inclinations. Such are, indeed, the difficulties meeting any effort to instigate economic and social reform in all countries. That they have been particularly great in a country with such a peculiar reluctance to interfere with people's liberty to do what they please, and with so little homogeneity—racially, culturally, economically, and in all other respects—is clear.

In the North, undoubtedly, nonviolent action along the Southern pattern, backed by the huge compounds of blacks in their segregated districts in the cities, could have broken down orderly administration and so forced changes. But that did not happen. King's attempts in Chicago to start large-scale direct action were not successful.

Instead, from around the middle of the 1960s, came the riots. Unplanned and undirected as policy actions, and not clearly aimed at any defintite reforms, they testified to the frustrations born in the black community. We are still as ignorant about why the riots began when they did as about why they stopped after 1968.

The effect of the riots on the black community was to demonstrate that the lives lost and the damage done overwhelmingly hurt almost only the blacks. Among thoughtful whites, the riots did focus attention on how bad the economic and social situation was for the blacks, or most of them—to which the Kerner Commission report gave testimony. At the same time the riots made many whites fearful and angry.

Whether the very high level of unemployment in the present economic crisis, particularly among black youths, may increase the risk of new riots in the cities is open to conjecture. With very few exceptions, nobody in the black community, North or South, has raised his voice urging violent action.

But undoubtedly there has been a new awakening of a black

nationalist spirit. Few or none of the ideologies formed and expressed in this line are original; they have had their counterparts thoughout American history. In *An American Dilemma* I saw them as counterreactions to the rationalizations given by whites of their treatment of black Americans, and I am inclined to stick to this view.

In a fully integrated American nation there would be little reason for black nationalism. In the existing situation black nationalism is, however, not only understandable but must to an extent be considered curative in nature. Thus a forceful confirmation that "black is beautiful" is a healthy reaction, and so is the resistance against giving up all cultural traits that have evolved from their special history.

As the Southern Black Revolt was running its course toward success in establishing equal formal rights also in the South, the two regions came to be more on a par. In the South as in the North what remains in order to establish real equality of opportunities is now to overcome that social system which holds the blacks down—there as in the North. The South is still poorer, its taxation more regressive, and its social services more niggardly. But the revolutionary changes already undergone may have given the South more of a momentum for reform.

It is my impression that the white South is gradually overcoming the feelings of guilt and inferiority which stemmed from the experience of holding on to outworn racial dogmas, being constantly attacked, and having to fight a losing battle. Now there is often expressed, sometimes from unexpected quarters, positive pride in the results of the Black Revolt and positive appreciation of the black political leaders now emerging to play their role in public policy and administration. They are in a sense "new," as the vote for the black is new, and they can plan their actions without being tied down by earlier alignments and commitments.

If this trend continues, it would imply the final victory of the Southern white liberals and at the same time the restoration of a healthy self-confidence, which the South has not experienced for much more than a century.

Since *An American Dilemma* we have had ever more abundantly performed opinion studies, many of them focusing on the problem of how blacks and whites view each other. Without having the opportunity in this context to enter into the many complexities that are raised, I want to stress that there is revealed a consistent trend, not broken by the race riots, of whites having steadily less unfavorable views of blacks: their intelligence, industriousness, ambitions, morality, etc. This trend of change is recorded also for whites in the South, though rising from a lower level and continuously remaining somewhat behind. Similar trends have been recorded in regard to opinions on policy issues: segregation or not in public transportation, separate or integrated schools, etc.

A disturbing fact, however, is that the answers have not been so positive when the questions were formulated in less general and more specific and personal terms; for example, whether one would send his own children to an integrated school. Also disturbing is that when people were asked what they believed about other white's opinions, both in the South and in the North, people regularly gave much higher estimates of racial prejudices prevalent in their communities than what would be extrapolated from their own opinions. This cannot simply be ignorance about other people—and ignorance is in any case regularly opportunistic. Does it reveal that under the strain of the activization of the ideals in the national purpose, which has been proceeding, ordinary people pretend to be more idealistic than they really are?

In any case, this new opinion research testifies that there has been a huge and continuous change in white people's *public* opinions about blacks and their rights. Even when these public opinions do not correspond to propensities to act, or not to act, *privately* in various situations in life, they do have their importance. For one thing, they might steer actions in the sphere of public policy.

Under the influences of the forces reflected in the opinion studies, there has actually been a continuous wave of legislation against discrimination, particularly in the labor market. Sometimes the implementation of these new laws has been fortified by the setting up of administrative agencies empowered to bring lawsuits against employers who can be proved to have broken them. All sorts of "affirmative action" have been prescribed.

Quite in line with the ideals of the national purpose, this new political and legislative activity has not been restricted to protecting the rights of blacks only, but has generally applied to "minority groups." A more recent development is that the protective shield has also been raised to defend the rights to equality for women.

So far as the blacks are concerned, but even more generally, these new efforts are mainly of practical importance for the upper and middle classes of professionals and business employees. Only to some extent is the working class affected, primarily the more steadily employed workers gaining entrance into trade unions. That affirmative action does not give much help to the underclass of blacks—or other groups—in the slums where unemployment and subemployment are high is clear. It is the ultimate demand of a Welfare State—to provide a minimum level of living and security for *all* citizens—which is not being met by these otherwise important reforms.

In the 1930s Franklin D. Roosevelt had stressed, as a moral issue, the need for economic reform. This was right in line with the meaning of the national purpose. By pronouncing "freedom from want" a part of "liberty," Roosevelt had, in fact, reinterpreted the national purpose, including in it the rights of all Americans to a decent living standard and a measure of security. Although this programmatic commitment went far beyond accomplishment, then even more than now, the United States had thus been established as moving toward becoming a Welfare State.

Since Roosevelt there have been many social reforms in America. But from the beginning they have showed a tendency to stop above the reach of the poorest and most needy. Even with the gradual increase over the years in the numbers of those who benefited from reforms in such areas as minimum wages, social insurance, housing, health care, and so on, such programs still do not usually reach down to the underclass.

For example, one of President Roosevelt's most consequential policy initiatives was the Social Security Act of 1935. Of crucial importance for the development of income maintenance policies in the United States was his choice to follow the line of thinking of Bismarck and Lloyd George, who had conceived the social problem as *eine Arbeiterfrage*, concerning only those employed in the labor market and not endeavoring to cover the nation as a whole.

The social security system in the United States thereafter has been given an ever wider coverage until it now extends over perhaps 90 percent of the labor force. Protection for certain risks other than old age and unemployment has also been more or less adequately provided for by additions to the system. But the bulk of the tremendous sums being transferred is transmitted through a compulsory insurance system, based upon a private insurance model, kept outside the state and federal budgets, and paid for by regressive payroll charges. The main deficiency of this system from the point of view of social policy goals is, however, that it only covers workers having a decent and reasonably steady job. From the major aid schemes within this system are excluded the whole underclass of the more permanently unemployed and the "subemployed," indeed all those not in the mainstream of economic life.

Behind the continuing bias in American social reforms lies an ideological difference between the United States and the more advanced welfare states. In these other countries, at least since the 1930s, the theory has been that well-planned social reforms are a profitable investment, improving the quality and thus the productivity of people and also precluding future public and private expenditures. That theory is almost missing in the United States where social reforms are mostly looked upon simply as public expenditures, which might be justified on grounds of justice. The lack of sufficient consideration of the investment aspect of social reforms is perhaps understandable in the United States because of the extreme wretchedness of the situation for the large underclass in the slums—a situation partly caused by the extraordinarily high levels of unemployment and subemployment but also by the fact that many social reforms stop above the reach of that underclass.

Every country, even the most advanced welfare state, needs to have possibilities to give additional public assistance to individuals and families who for various reasons have come into economic difficulty. With the incompleteness of the American system for income maintenance and the inadequacy of other equalizing social policies, supervised public assistance has had to expand in an incomparable measure, but nevertheless remains inadequate to meet the needs of the poor. I believe it is important to stress the relation between the shortcomings of what is done for equality and welfare normally, without necessitating so much interference in private lives, and the expansion of supervised public assistance. The public assistance system is generally acknowledged to be muddled, relatively expensive, humiliating, unfair, and conducive to many unfortunate effects on its clientele.

After World War II Americans, like people in other rich countries, felt that the government should take responsibility for economic policies that would secure full employment for all workers. Immediately after the war the Senate passed, with no negative votes, a Full Employment Bill specifying that

all Americans able to work and seeking work have the right to useful, remunerative, regular, and full-time employment, and it is the policy of the United States to assure the existence at all times of sufficient employment opportunities to enable all Americans . . . freely to exercise this right.

The more conservative House of Representatives saw to it that the final legislation of 1946 shifted the government commitment downward toward maintenance of "maximal" employment in a way "consistent with its needs and obligations and other essential considerations of national policies."

In the beginning, the tolerable level of unemployment was spoken of as 3 percent, a level above what in other Western countries could be so considered. Later, without much debate, 4 percent unemployment came to be see as "maximal" and then as "full" employment. By 1975 a 6 percent unemployment rate was widely proposed as the "full employment" standard and, of course, actual unemployment reached higher levels. Unemployment rates have regularly been about double as high for blacks as for whites, the difference tending to rise in recessions and decrease in stable times.

Furthermore, the continually quoted figures for unemployment do not include those who are involuntarily in part-time work. Neither are unemployed workers included who are not actively seeking work because they find it hopeless. There are also workers whose full-time work is so low paid that they remain impoverished. This is what is called "subemployment," striking especially blacks, youths, married women, and older workers.

Even if we stick to the grossly inadequate official unemployment statistics, it is evident that America has shown a remarkable tolerance for unemployment. In spite of the high unemployment rates the great majority of workers do always have employment. Moreover, even most of those workers who are officially classified as unemployed get paid unemployment insurance benefits through the social security system for a rather long, and recently prolonged, period. These in America are often called the "middle class." High unemployment only becomes intolerable for those unemployed workers who fall outside the social security system and for all subemployed, those I call the "underclass."

It is a disturbing thought that by stretching out unemployment insurance to all the more regularly employed workers the remarkable and extraodinary tolerance of high rates of unemployment has been made more possible politically. At the same time there has developed a gulf between that "middle class" and the underclass. In particular the distance to the welfare clientele has widened. It is not difficult to descry among this "middle class" suspiciousness that many welfare recipients are frauds and unwilling to work.

Nobody who has read the preceding pages can doubt that I attach importance to ideals for economic, social, and political development—if they are rooted in the hearts of people and especially if, as in America, they are inscribed in constitutional documents. But the ideals need to be activated by pressure from below. History does not give examples of privileged groups climbing down from their privileges and opening up their monopolies, except under such pressure.

The successful Black Revolt in the South gave an example of how pressure from a unified black community could activate ideals in the national purpose so that they became social forces for change. I remember from that time an article in the *Washington Post* raising the question whether the example demonstrated so

successfully by the blacks would cause other unprivileged groups
to organize themselves for mass action, join the blacks and together bring about greater equality in America. But the Black Revolt, in spite of its broad appeal to solidarity with other groups, did
not generate a unified movement of people in the lower classes to
demand more equality. Instead we experienced the "white backlash."

The more fundamental causes of the very apparent lack of
solidarity among people of the lower classes in America are rooted
in the fact that the nation, composed of immigrants and the de-
scendants of immigrants, is not yet a well-integrated society, and
less so among the lower classes, in which I include all under the
upper class—lower-level professionals; small-scale, often self-em-
ployed business entrepreneurs; the working class, and the underclass. The history of the nation has continuously fragmented
the lower classes, split in racial, ethnic, cultural, liguistic, and religious subgroups. Superimposed on this fragmentation is the systematically induced difference in economic advantages from social
policies referred to above.

Lacking solidarity, the lower classes have not generated unified, broadly based and, therefore, effective mass organizations.
There has generally been a remarkable lack of widely encompass-
ing, self-generating, self-disciplined, organized and protracted
people's movements. The ununified lower classes which form the
great majority of the nation are accustomed to remaining static and
receptive and often struggling amongst themselves. The rate of
participation in elections has, in spite of very high levels of publicity and propaganda, remained astonishingly low. The nonvoters
are predominantly people in the lower classes.

"Movements" prominent in other Western countries, and especially in the advanced welfare states, are mostly conspicuous by
their absence or weakness in the United States. American trade
unions, which leave three-quarters of the workers unorganized, do
not look upon themselves as a spearheads of social reform movement. There has never been much of a cooperative movement in
America. They, as well as lobby organizations working in Washington for the consumer's interests, have had little backing from

broad strata of the people, joining together in order to protect their common interests. There is still hardly any concerted drive for self-education in civic affairs by people themselves in the lower strata, e. g., by forming study groups within the trade unions or in neighborhood blocks. There is evidently no spontaneous mass desire for knowledge as a collective means of achieving independence and power.

This situation contrasts with that of Northwestern Europe, where labor parties are the final outcome of much more than a century of great and influential people's movements: general suffrage, temperance, cooperative, trade union adult education, and the nonconformist religious movements. All of these were genuine mass movements, even if individuals from the upper classes joined them and often constituted part of the leadership. Together they gradually created a social infrastructure of a broadly based activist cooperation. As organized and protracted mass movements they were in a sense self-generating, stemming from group solidarity. Thus they tended to produce what in the most advanced welfare states, particularly Sweden, has been call a "service democracy"— one in which all political parties have to compete with each other in proposing further development of new social reforms.

When the air went out of the "unconditional war against poverty" and the "Great Society" balloons, immediate causes were, of course, the Vietnam War, which absorbed both financial resources and the interest of people in Washington and, at the end, President Nixon's opposition. But a more basic reason was that the whole effort—once reflected in an explosion of books, articles and conferences at many universities, and the appearance of increasingly pertinent statistics on poverty—was never effectively supported by pressure from below. The attempts in many of the projects to stimulate participation by the poor in their own interest were largely ineffective.

Taking the broader view, the conditions of life and work of the blacks in America have improved during the last thirty-five years. The advance has had setbacks and been uneven. The positive results are more pronounced for the professional middle class and, to an extent, for the regular working class, as the trade unions have gradually been opened. Blacks' facilities for health, education, housing have been improving, although segregation and discrimination have not been entirely broken—in housing hardly at all. Jim Crow in the South, however, has crumpled and disappeared. Even there the blacks are now voting, and the general trend both there and in the North has been that they are using their voting power increasingly to further their interests effectively.

As blacks have become actors on both the national and the local scenes, they have had to consider strategy and tactics. The problem of race relations is no longer merely a "white man's problem" as I could realistically characterize it thirty-five years ago. Even though the majority of whites still have most of the power, blacks, like whites, are now facing the dilemma, and their own choice of actions has considerable influence on the development of race relations.

Meanwhile the various economic and social reforms moving the United States toward becoming a welfare state have tended to fall short of reaching the poorest and most needy. Despite the trend toward a continual widening downward of the groups being aided, reforms do not reach down to the underclass. And, even if only between one-quarter and one-third of all the poor in America are black, they are a much bigger proportion of the blacks than of other groups. Especially in the black ghettos of the big cities, all too many young people are left to grow up without hope.

With all efforts in the field of education which have particularly favored the blacks, America is still far from realizing equality of educational opportunity for all poor children and youths. And in spite of medicare and medicaid and other federal, state, and local undertakings, health policies still remain a patchwork and are unfortunately also tarnished by much exploitation and even corruption, particularly when dealing wih the poor. Preventive medicine is, relatively speaking, underdeveloped. In international statistics on morbidity and mortality this inadequacy even shows up in high average rates.

On the other hand, it should be added that there seems to have evolved a rather commonly shared opinion in Congress that efforts have to be made to give all Americans access to medical care, even if opinions differ as to how a comprehensive health reform can be accomplished. The equally commonly shared dissatisfaction with the present system of closely supervised public assistance to the very poorest should also promise a fundamental reform which in one way or another will have to afford more effective income maintenance to the welfare clientele and with less intrusion on their privacy. For such a reform to be effective it has to be supplemented by special social welfare policies in the interest of the old and the children as well as all the various categories of handicapped people.

Taking an overall view, I find confirmation of my belief of thirty-five years ago that the ideals in the national purpose are given more than lip service and that in the longer run they have determined the trend of development in America. Even though this development has still left the nation far away from fully accepting the ideals of the national purpose as commitments, I cannot believe that America has come to the end of its long march to become a more perfect union.

6.

CIVIL RIGHTS AND SELF-GOVERNMENT

In 1776 "Our fathers brought forth on this continent, a new nation," President Lincoln said, "conceived in Liberty, and dedicated to the proposition that all men are created equal." In those words, President Lincoln proclaimed for all time the essential character of American constitutional government.

At the close of his Gettysburg address, Lincoln returned to his theme that the United States was a new nation, a different nation, and he hoped "that government of the people, by the people, for the people, shall not perish from the earth."

During the Impeachment Inquiry of 1974, Barbara Jordan expressed a different view. Referring to the Preamble to the Constitution, Ms. Jordan said:

> We the people, it's a very eloquent beginning. But when the document was completed on the 17th of September in 1787, I was not included in that we the people. I felt somehow for many years that George Washington and Alexander Hamilton just left me out by mistake. But through the process of amendment, interpretation, and court decisions, I have finally been included in we the people.

Since 1976 is a year of celebration, it seems appropriate to examine how all the people became part of we the people.

It may be too soon to examine these developments. The events are too recent. We need time to place events side by side; time to stand back and examine and reexamine these events from different perspectives before making any judgements.

Nevertheless, for a good part of the period I was involved in some of the events, and I want to try to tell and to try to understand what has happened and what it means.

Following World War II, the United States appeared to stand at the zenith of its power. We had just won a great war, a war in which technology, productivity, and capacity for massive organization had played an important part. Thereafter, we undertook to help rebuild Western Europe. We accepted the challenge of the competing totalitarian systems who insisted that, in due course, they would bury us. We believed we were ready to fight a long cold war of survival.

Although the preceding period, from 1920 to 1950, had been a time when the forces of totalitarian government, the antithesis of constitutional self-government, seemed on the rise, our system of self-government appeared to be very strong. But it was not.

Within the United States there existed a caste system—a system which doomed to second-class status over 10 percent of our people. This condition undercut basic principles of self-government, and brought into question our nation's long-term chance of survival. A good place to begin is to describe the American caste system as I found it.

During the summer of 1960, as a new attorney in the Civil Rights Division of the Department of Justice, I was sent to Hayward and Fayette counties in southwestern Tennessee. This was six years after the Supreme Court's crucial school desegregation decision; three years after Little Rock; three years after the passage of the first federal civil rights legislation since Reconstruction; three or four months after the first sit-in in North Carolina.

In those two rural Tennessee counties, where the majority of the people were black, the local white leadership, who were prosperous cotton farmers and their merchants, bankers, and lawyers, had embarked on a systematic program of evicting hundreds of black sharecroppers from the land. Black families were asked to move from homes on land which they had sharecropped for years. This concerted program was undertaken solely because a small group of local blacks had formed a Civic Improvement League whose purpose was to encourage people to register and vote. Carried out in the winter time, the program was cruel and savage.

This program was based on the premise that the majority of the American people and their chosen representatives would tolerate illegal conduct in states or counties where equal participation by blacks might mean that blacks would actually share in American constitutional self-government.

Around the end of 1960, after the Justice Department had litigated these first cases against some 150 white residents of Hayward and Fayette counties, I drove two hundred miles south through the Mississippi Delta, across the Mississippi River to East Carroll Parish, Louisiana, a delta county of cotton farms and small towns. Again, the majority of the people who lived there were blacks.

There I listened to the problems of Francis Joseph Atlas, age fifty-six. He was a black farmer. He owned sixty-five acres of land and rented some more. He raised cotton, soybeans, small grains. He had twenty-four head of cattle. He had lived in East Carroll Parish all his life. He was a respected small farmer. He and his wife had raised twelve children: three school teachers; two sons in the Army; a daughter a nurse in Chicago; another son a transit company employee; three kids in college, two still at home.

Mr. Atlas was not registered to vote. He first tried in 1948, but he didn't get anywhere. Several years later, he tried again. He was told that the law required two qualified electors to identify him. No blacks were registered and none of Mr. Atlas' white friends felt they could afford to do it. A little later, a group of blacks filed suit in the Federal Court. It was not successful.

In 1959, he went to a meeting and talked to two gentlemen from the Civil Rights Commission. They were interested in the voting problems of blacks in East Carroll Parish. On September 22, 1960, Mr. Atlas received a subpoena to appear before the Civil

Rights Commission in New Orleans. On the Saturday before he testified he had taken his first truckload of cotton to the gin located two miles from his farm. He drove the wagon under the sucker and the cotton was ginned.

On September 27, Mr. Atlas went to New Orleans to testify about his difficulties in attempting to register to vote. His testimony received publicity in both the New Orleans and Monroe papers.

The next evening the sheriff came to Mr. Atlas' home. He came up on the porch and told Mr. Atlas that the ginners said: "Don't bring no more cotton to their gins." Mr. Atlas asked why, and the sheriff said, "civil rights."

Thereafter Mr. Atlas tried to find out the reason. All his white friends would tell him was that he had done something that was not in the best interest of the parish.

Mr. Atlas couldn't get gas to heat his home. His local suppliers turned his open accounts over to lawyers. He was sued. When I saw Mr. Atlas in early January he had already lost part of his crops. With the ordinary channels of business in the parish closed to him, and with his credit cut off, he faced a situation where he could not continue to operate his farm. Mr. Atlas was sure that the squeeze he had been put in would, unless stopped, keep many black citizens from attempting to vote. He told me that already he had noticed that his black friends in East Carroll seemed afraid to know him—"They shake my hand quickly and walk on by."

The Justice Department was able to get Mr. Atlas' cotton ginned, but what was more to the point, we began to appreciate the relentless determination of white people to maintain the caste system.

Within a month, I had seen similar situations repeated in Macon and Bullock counties, Alabama. The purpose was always the same. Blacks who tried to register to vote were prevented from registering or applications were limited by the threat of economic sanctions.

It was not a pretty picture. The rural blacks we saw were examples of virtue—strong, energetic, careful, loyal, honest, capable of self-sacrifice, decent. The whites, locked together, determined, sometimes mean, more often frightened, directed most of their energy toward keeping blacks in their second-class status.

During the spring and summer of 1961, I spent time in southwest Mississippi. There the Student Non-Violent Coordinating Committee had come to encourage local blacks to register. The response of the white people was violent. Northern black students were arrested or beaten, local blacks were intimidated. One local black farmer was killed, allegedly for threatening a Mississippi state senator with a tire iron. We were not able to do much about it.

As I crossed and recrossed Georgia, Alabama, Mississippi, and Louisiana in the months thereafter, I found a complex legal and social network designed to preserve the caste system. The means used were official corruption and official and unofficial intimidation.

In Alabama, Louisiana, and Mississippi the caste system was reflected in the laws of the individual states. The scheme was not haphazard. Almost every activity was affected.

A black's birth certificate so identified him. He lived on a segregated street, he was segregated in parks and playgrounds. Until 1960 almost all blacks attended segregated schools. As an adult, a black was segregated at all entertainment functions. Mixed social functions were banned. At work, the blacks ate separately and used separate sanitary facilities. A black could not marry outside of his race. Institutions for the blind and deaf were segregated. Prisons were segregated. When a black died, his death was attested by a certificate identifying him by race. And he was buried in a segregated cemetery.

An enormous amount of human energy went into maintaining the caste system. One means used was to restrict the vote to white residents only. This is the way it had been for a long time. Judge John Minor Wisdom described this effort in the landmark 1963 case of *United States v. Louisiana*:

> A wall stands in Louisiana between registered voters and unregistered, eligible Negro voters.[1]

Judge Wisdom described how this wall had been built:

> The Louisiana Codes Noir of Colonial times and the Black Codes of the eighteen sixties; the pre-Civil War denial of the vote to Negroes,

even to wealthy and educated free men of color; the ebb and flow of
Negro rights in the Constitutions of 1864 and 1868; the 1879 transfer
of political power from police juries and the legislature to the
Governor; the close election of 1892 and the 1896 victory for white
supremacy; the grandfather clause and the complicated registration
application form in the Constitution of 1898; the invalidity of the
grandfather clause and the consequent resort to Mississippi's
understanding and interpretation clause; the effectiveness of the
white primary . . . the invalidity of the white primary and the
consequent need to revive enforcement of the interpretation test; the
White League and the Citizens' Councils; . . . the Battle of Liberty
Place in 1874 and the Ouachita voting purge of 1956—these are all
related members of a series, all reactions to the same dynamics that
produced the interpretation test and speak eloquently of its purpose.
. . . the interpretation test is another grandfather clause. Its purpose is
rooted in the same history. It has the same objective the delegates to
the Constitutional convention of 1898 envisaged for the grandfather
clause. It is capable of producing the same effective disfranchisement
of Negroes today that the grandfather clause produced sixty-five
years ago.[2]

There was only one conclusion that one could draw from this.
Less than twenty years ago, there existed in these United States a
rigid caste system that affected ten million black people who lived
in the Southern states and probably millions more who had moved
North in the hope of avoiding it. But it affected more people than
that. It affected all of us who purported to believe that we lived
under a constitutional system of self-government.

In the years following 1960, efforts within the United States
were increased to do away with the caste system. With regard to
the right to vote, several institutions, groups, and individuals converged to meet this same crisis in American society.

You know the individuals and groups as well as I. Bob Moses
and the Student Non-violent Coordinating Committee (SNCC); Dr.
King and Southern Christian Leadership Conference (SCLS); Dave
Dennis and James Farmer of Congress for Racial Equality (CORE);
their supporters such as the Southern Regional Council; the northern ministers and the legions of individuals in the academic community; and of course, the federal government. The efforts of all
these institutions, groups, and individuals were not a unified joint
endeavor, but were instead complementary. Each contributed

something individual toward the effort. Each discovered a sphere in which it would work most effectively. Each developed a distinctive style. Yet there was confidence that all believed it must be and it could be demonstrated that American people of every race and color had an equal right to share in the processes of self-government.

Since we are measuring the performance of our constitutional system, I want to focus on the efforts of the three branches of the federal government to insure the right to vote. I want, first, to examine the judicial record. The only place to begin is with the United States courts in the Fifth Circuit, for the performance of certain judges in that circuit will be remembered with advantage for as long as our nation lives.

The territory of this circuit stretches from Texas through Florida. In 1960 there were seven Courts of Appeals judges, and about twenty District Court judges, each of whom, pursuant to the Constitution, held a lifetime appointment.

In 1960 there were four judges on the Fifth Circuit Court of Appeals and one District Court judge who took the leadership in deciding civil rights cases and in explaining the decisions clearly and in words that were to be remembered. The four judges on the Court of Appeals were Judge Elbert P. Tuttle of Georgia, Judge Richard T. Rives of Alabama, Judge John Minor Wisdom of Louisiana, and Judge John R. Brown of Texas. The District Court Judge was Frank M. Johnson of Montgomery, Alabama.

Below the Supreme Court the federal judicial selection process is weighted so that the judges reflect the attitudes of the people who vote in the states in which they live. District Court appointments, at least, traditionally must have the approval of both senators from the state before the Senate will confirm them. At the same time, the federal judges were the officials designated by law to enforce the Voting Rights acts of 1957 and 1960.

These five judges lived within the caste society. They were different; they came from different backgrounds and the traditions of the society may have weighed more heavily on one than on another, but each of them had many friends and life-long loyalties to the region. It would not have been predictable that the Fifth

Circuit of the federal court system would become the leader in disturbing the caste system. It was to these five judges that the Justice Department turned to find the facts and declare the law.

Early in 1961, Judge Frank M. Johnson ordered the Macon County, Alabama, registrars to permit blacks to register to vote without passing any test of literacy or understanding. The rationale: white voters had been registered on that basis for years.[3]

Several months later Judge Rives decided a case where the United States sought to enjoin a Mississippi criminal prosecution of a voter registration worker who was assaulted by the Walthall County registrar when he accompanied two elderly black residents to the courthouse to register. Speaking for a majority of the court, Judge Rives said:

> The foundation of our form of government is the consent of the governed. Whenever any person interferes with the right of any other person to vote, he acts like a political termite to destroy a part of that foundation. . . . Eradication of political termites, or at least checking their activities, is necessary to prevent irreparable damage to our government.[4]

Judge Tuttle of Georgia, the chief judge of the Fifth Circuit, possessed the capacity and the patience not only to pore carefully through the records in the voting cases that came to his court for review, but also to outlast the recalcitrant district judges who intended to maintain the status quo. He also had to ability to explain in clear, detailed, not-to-be misunderstood language exactly what methods the local white officials had used to keep blacks from voting, and then spell out what had to be done and why in order to remedy the situation.

Judge Tuttle wished he could have done more. I remember hearing him speak to Burke Marshall, then the Assistant Attorney General for Civil Rights, at a hearing before the full panel of Appeals Court judges when James Meredith sought orders directing the governor of Mississippi to cease interfering with his admission to the University of Mississippi. He said:

> I think I do state the views of the Court that the Court has practically exhausted its powers in the circumstances. I am sure it is a planned policy of our government that a Court have no power to execute its

orders . . . . the Court feels that the time has come . . . when the burden now falls on the Executive Branch of the Government. Now [Mr. Marshall] will you . . . indicate, if you can, what can be done by the Executive Department to see that the Court's orders are carried out.[5]

Assistant Attorney General Burke Marshall replied in a way that foreshadowed the ultimate resolution the problem of massive racial discrimination in voting across the South. By this I mean the necessity that the three co-equal branches of the federal government function together, each in its own sphere of power, if the federal government is to function effectively. In this instance Mr. Marshall spoke for the Executive Branch when he replied:

We recognize the responsibility of the Executive Branch of the Government . . . to enforce the orders of the Court. . . .We also have a responsibility to make every effort to enforce the orders of the Court in a way that is least disruptive of the national interest, and when we are dealing with a state, we want to give the state every opportunity . . . to cooperate with the Court and the Federal Government in seeing that the orders are obeyed. . . .We have attempted to proceed in a responsible fashion, giving every opportunity first to the University and then to the government of the State of Mississippi to meet their responsibilities.[6]

At the same time Mr. Marshall's words underlined the importance of straightforwardness and clarity in committing the use of federal power:

Now . . . despite every attempt that we have made to have the order of the Court respected and obeyed voluntarily . . . those efforts have thus far failed, and it appears that stronger efforts are going to have to be made to enforce the order of the Court . . . . There is no question but that the Executive Branch of the Government will use whatever force, physical force, is required, if that is required, to enforce the order of the Court. . . .That task will be easier and the country will be better off if by the order of this Court we can yet bring the state officials . . . to a recognition of their responsibilities to cooperate with us instead of opposing us in accomplishing this purpose.[7]

By the end of 1964, due to the courage and leadership of these five judges, discriminatory administration of voting qualifications had been found in all eight Alabama cases, in all nine Louisiana cases, and in all nine Mississippi cases which had gone to final judgment. In the process of rendering these decisions Judge Wisdom had spelled out the disgraceful history of state actions in Louisiana in keeping blacks from voting, and Judge Brown had done the same for Mississippi. In *U. S. v. Mississippi*, Judge Brown wrote:

> . . . history tells us that no political institution is indestructible. If it is to survive, it must save itself from destruction. It is the peril of destruction which is what this case is all about.[8]

Judge Brown wrote that this was a controversy between all citizens of the United States and the state of Mississippi. He examined the laws of Mississippi and showed that its constitutional provisions and the implementing statutory laws regulating registration of voters came into being—and were maintained—"out of a purpose by the organized state to deny Negroes the right to vote."

Judge Brown characterized Mississippi's racial policy, as Judge Wisdom had done before him, as "a steelhard, inflexible, undeviating official policy of segregation."[9] Judge Brown concluded as follows:

> Discrimination against Negroes . . . has happened because it was meant to happen. To eradicate this evil, the attack . . . may be made by a frontal assault on the whole structure.[10]

In spite of the rulings of the Fifth Circuit, by early 1964, Burke Marshall, the Assistant Attorney General who directed the government's attack on the caste system, began to talk pessimistically about the future.

At his Columbia University Speranza Lecture Marshall reported that the federal government in seven years' time had demonstrated an inability to make significant advances in making the right to vote real in the deep South.[11] Mr. Marshall could not find any structural reason in our constitutional system to suggest that the basic problem was beyond solution. But he was concerned with time, and he foresaw as a possibility a mass of litigation in the federal courts which would take years to resolve.

He pointed out that in 1963 President Kennedy had suggested legislation which would temporarily alter the degree of state control over the registration process in the most difficult areas. But Congress had been unwilling to accept this intrusion in established state control.

In concluding his lecture Mr. Marshall warned of the growing strain on the federal structure in the Deep South and added:

Moreover the domestic tranquility is at stake, for the Negro cause against discrimination is indivisible. When Negroes are excluded from participation in their government in even one county, and state authority is twisted to allow it, while federal authority appears powerless to take effective steps, the gulf between Negroes and whites everywhere is widened, and the chance of racial conflict increased. At the least, the generation of students which sees this happen are to some extent losing faith in their government, with consequences for the future that cannot be foreseen.[12]

During the winter of 1963-64 the Student Non-Violent Coordinating Committee organized northern white students into a program called Mississippi Summer. These students planned to work in Mississippi on voter registration. Early in the summer, three young men were murdered in Neshoba County, Mississippi. Two of them, James Schwerner and Andrew Goodman, were from New York. That ultimate crime of violence was just one of a number of serious, unlawful acts and practices that had been inflicted on blacks and their supporters during the years I spent in the South.

I can't begin to describe what it was like for us, as federal law enforcement officials, to witness this. Each of us reacted in his or her own way. For many there didn't seem to be anything to do except to move ahead, as lawyers, with more and more voting cases to help the Fifth Circuit all that we could.

I don't intend to dwell on that aspect of this chapter in American history. But we should not forget the suffering that many individuals and their families experienced during those times.

In spite of the resistance, in spite of the frustrations, I never lost hope that our system of self-government would somehow reach a point where in fact all men were equal in their right to participate in the processes of government. But I didn't know how or when it would happen.

It began to happen in 1965; the place we associate it with is Selma, Dallas County, Alabama.

I had first gone to Selma in February of 1961. At that time there was a local organization of blacks in Selma which was trying to break down the barriers to voting. Several months later the first voting case brought by the Kennedy administration was filed against the registrars of Dallas County. The next year SNCC opened a field office in Selma, and worked there from then on.

During the next four years Civil Rights Division attorneys spent more time in Dallas County than in any other county in the South. Jim Clark was the sheriff and he was unbending in his commitment to segregation. The registrars and all other county officials behaved likewise.

Late in 1964 Dr. King and his SCLC organization came to Selma. Out of this convergence of forces came a series of events which culminated in the incident at the Selma Bridge, when mounted state police dispersed, with clubs and tear gas, a number of blacks on their way to the state capitol in Montgomery to present their grievances to the governor. After this episode came the Voting Rights Act of 1965.

The record of the Voting Rights Act of 1965 illustrates the strength and capacity of our system of constitutional self-government.

Between March 15, 1965, when President Lyndon B. Johnson first went before a joint session of the Congress, and June 1966, the three coequal branches of the federal government worked independently but in harmony to make the Fifteenth Amendment mean what it says.

On March 15 President Johnson appeared before a joint session of the Congress. He called upon Congress to meet the challenge to "the values and the purposes and the meaning" of our nation. He said that if we as a people were unequal to the issue of equal rights for American blacks we will have failed as a people and as a nation. He urged Congress to work long hours, nights and weekends to pass the bill, and reminded them that they faced the harsh judgement of history for their action.[13]

On March 18 a bill entitled "The Voting Rights Act of 1965" was introduced. On the same day Attorney General Nicholas Katzenbach appeared before the House Judiciary Committee to testify in detail about the bill. He spelled out how the registration process in the South had been perverted to test "not literacy, not ability, not understanding—but race." He explained the basic provision of the bill which suspended all tests in six Southern states and thirty four counties in North Carolina and empowered the Attorney General to send registrars into any county where, in his judgment, the appointment of registrars was necessary to enforce the guarantees of the Fifteenth Amendment.[14]

By August 6, 1965, Congress had acted and the President had signed the legislation. In acting, Congress added a very important provision to the bill. Section 8 provided that in every county where federal examiners had been assigned, the Attorney General might assign federal observers to any polling place within the county to see that all persons who were entitled to vote were permitted to vote and have their votes properly counted.

The Act was given meaning on the day of the signing ceremony. There President Johnson set the tempo when he said:

I intend to act with dispatch in enforcing this Act. . .

Tomorrow at 1:00 P. M. the Attorney General has been directed to file a lawsuit challenging the constitutionality of the poll tax in the State of Mississippi. . .

By Tuesday morning, trained federal examiners will be at work registering eligible men and women in 10 or 15 counties.

And on that same day, next Tuesday additional poll tax suits will be filed in the states of Texas, Alabama, and Virginia.[15]

On the Monday following the passage of the Voting Rights Act, the Civil Service Commission announced that registration offices would be open in nine counties in three states. On the first day that these offices were open, 1,144 blacks registered. During the first week, 9,845 blacks registered. By the first of the year there were thirty-six counties where federal officials were operating and 79,815 blacks had been registered. During the same period local officials in the five states of the Deep South registered 215,000 blacks—the direct result of voluntary compliance by local officials.

This compliance did not occur by chance. On the day following the passage of the Act, Attorney General Katzenbach wrote to the 650 registration officials. He explained the provisions of the statute and told them that his decision to appoint examiners would be made when it was clear that past denials of the right to vote justified it, or where present compliance with federal law was insufficient to assure prompt registration of all eligible citizens.

During the first year, FBI agents checked voter registration books in every county for the five-state area on a weekly basis. Young attorneys in the Civil Rights Division spent long days in rural counties in the South explaining the law to local officials and to black citizens and bringing situations of noncompliance to the attention of the Attorney General.

On March 7, 1966, the Supreme Court upheld the validity of the Voting Rights Act, by saying:

> After enduring nearly a century of widespread resistance to the Fifteenth Amendment, Congress has marshalled an array of potent weapons against the evil, with authority to the Attorney General to employ them effectively. . . . Hopefully, millions of nonwhite persons will now be able to participate for the first time on an equal basis in the government under which they live.[16]

On May 3, 1966, the first post-Voting Rights Act primary election arrived. Dallas County, Alabama, was the test county. The key race was for sheriff. The contestants were Jim Clark, the sheriff, and Wilson Baker, the sensible, moderate police chief of the City of Selma.

I was in Selma that day. It was a beautiful day. Within fifteen minutes after the polls opened, you felt a movement of people toward the polls. Near the federal courthouse in Selma, well-dressed black men and women could be seen walking to the polls. In the public housing area, where the Selma march began, by 8:15 A. M. There was a line outside the polling place of at least 350 black people. For most it was the first time they had voted in their lives. Across town in another black neighborhood where the streets were unpaved and the houses unpainted, there was the same movement of people toward the polls.

In rural Dallas County, some eighteen miles from Selma, in the little town of Orville (a town consisting of a closed bank, a post office, a general store, a drug store, a town hall, a machine shop or two) there were four polling places. At 9:30 around the polling places the streets were full of blacks. These were the rural people. None had ever voted before. In those four polling places over five hundred of some seven hundred registered blacks voted that day.

That night the returns in Dallas County came in very slowly.

South, if a black expected to be elected to a political office, he had to have white support. If a white politician expected to have a career in elective politics, he had to have black support.

In 1965 through 1967 efforts were begun to reform jury selection in the South. The government began to press hard for convictions of white persons who had conspired to harm blacks or other whites who had tried to break the caste system. Convictions resulted in some of the cases. For the first time our system of administration of justice started to work equally.

As Jimmy Breslin said in reporting on the conviction of three Klansmen who murdered Mrs. Liuzzo on the Selma-Montgomery highway following the end of the Selma-Montgomery march:

> It worked in Alabama last week for the first time. But that meant that it worked in California, in Watts, and in Paradise Valley in Detroit and in Harlem in New York. For every time a Klu Klux Klansman walks out of a courtroom free in the South, there are Negroes in the cities of the North who look at the laws and say the hell with them.[18]

But during the same period other events far overshadowed the corrections that the nation was finally making to its system of self-government.

In the years that followed 1965 the central events were riots and disorders, with a resulting hostility and bitterness toward our system of self-government. This was the consequences of 190 years of the caste system and the undeclared war in Vietnam.

At the end of 1967 I left the Justice Department to work in Bedford-Stuyvesant, an area in central Brooklyn where 400,000 blacks live. There I saw that blacks in the North had been subjected to a caste system similar to that in the South. More subtle, perhaps, more indirect, perhaps; but the effect was the same.

At the same time I saw black people who were confident that they could organize, participate, and succeed as part of one national society.

Perhaps the most important fact that I came to accept was that it would take years before this nation would be able to correct the effects of the caste system. During that period I was not able to measure how much we had accomplished as a nation in establishing that government by the people encompassed all the people.

In 1974 after working as special counsel to the House Judiciary Committee during the Impeachment Inquiry, I came to appreciate what had been accomplished.

The members of the Judiciary Committee were a diverse group. There were many new young members. There were blacks and women among the members. There were representatives of inner cities, suburbs, rural areas, the South, the heartland and the Far West. There were liberals and conservatives, and liberals within liberals and conservatives within conservatives. Three members were ex-members of the FBI. One was a priest.

There were two Texas representatives, one white, one black. Both had been close to President Johnson. There was a wealthy California representative who had been the president of Americans for Democratic Action; a school janitor's son; a tough black from Detroit; a Phi Beta Kappa who had studied in London; a black veteran wounded in Korea; a Yale graduate who had been an Arkansas attorney general; a representative from South Carolina who was a World War II army lieutenant colonel at twenty-five; a Princeton Rhodes scholar of Greek ancestry; a scion of a big business family decorated in World War II; a Mormon missionary; a former mayor of Bangor, Maine; a Dutchess County, New York, representative whose father, grandfather, and great-grandfather had served in the House of Representatives; a former aide to Representative William M. Colmer of Mississippi; and a committee chairman from Newark, New Jersey.

As the people's representatives it fell to these men and women to define the impeachment process, to make a decision—a decision which would be accepted by what Chairman Peter Rodino termed "the vast majority of the American people."

For months I sat at the foot of the committee watching our representatives. I saw them insist that the House define their authority. I saw them study every available historical source on the meaning of "other high Crimes and Misdemeanors." I saw them enhance the credibility of their proceedings by foreclosing access to their own investigative files until the hearings convened.

I saw them work out an appropriate and practical way to conduct their hearings and to provide to the President fair notice and an opportunity to be heard. I saw them study and study and study the evidence in the case. And, like most Americans, I saw them debate the question. Most important, I saw them make up their minds.

At some time during the proceeding I realized I was watching part of a "we the people" government. Let me illustrate what I mean.

On the afternoon of July 25, 1974, during the debate on Article I of the Articles of Impeachment, Congressman Harold V. Froehlich's turn came to speak. Congressman Froehlich was a plain man, dressed in a blue suit, white shirt, with a full head of fiery red hair. His shirt was short-sleeved. His coat sleeves were pulled well up on his arms. He had the thick wrists of a factory worker or a farmer. He came from the same area of Wisconsin as had Senator Joseph McCarthy. He was a typical Wisconsin Fox River Valley German-American. He didn't sound very impressive as he began by saying that Americans were traveling an unknown path and that the American people were frightened.

He acknowledged he was a Republican and loyal to his party. He believed that for impeachment a grave offense was necessary. He believed the evidence must be strong. He believed that the mandate of the people in the presidential election should not be overturned except for the most compelling circumstances. He said that the one-million-dollar impeachment staff had looked into thousands of allegations and these were words, words, words, words. He said that slowly most of the charges against the President had faded away. At that point I was sure he was opposed to impeachment.

But then he said he was bothered about the obstruction of justice. He believed there was a plan to cover up which the President had adopted shortly after June 17. He said the purpose of it was plain: first, to save the President's administration from embarrassment; second, to save himself from losing votes in November; and third, to save some of his loyal aides. He talked about the flurry of activity between the 17th and 20th of June at Key Biscayne, in California, and in Washington. He said that the President could reasonably be expected to know what was going on. He said that this was a President who was concerned about the pictures on the wall and the salads at official dinners. He thought it strange that the President didn't demand a clear explanation. He talked about when the President had said to John Dean, "John, you have the right plan." Then he said, "I have concluded I must vote for the impeachment of my President." And his voice broke.[19]

That evening Congresswoman Barbara Jordan spoke. Her voice was resonant. She seemed to electrify the other members of the Committee and they listened. She talked about the evidence. She talked about the misuse of the CIA and the fact that the President had known that Republican money had been found in the possession of the arrested burglars, and of the past activities of E. Howard Hunt. She talked about the committee's subpoenas being outstanding and that the committee was sitting if the President wished to supply that material. She said at the beginning, shortly after the Watergate break-in, and continuing to the present time the President had made a series of public statements and engaged in a series of public actions designed to thwart the lawful investigation by government prosecutors. Moreover, Ms. Jordan said, "The President has made public announcements and assertions bearing on the Watergate case which the evidence will show he knew to be false." When she finished she said that if the impeachment process did not reach the offenses here then our eighteenth-century Constitution should by abandoned to a twentieth-century paper shredder.[20]

There you had it, a white representative and a black representative leading the debate on the same side of the ultimate constitutional question.

I can still see the members, for example, those who sat on my left near the side of the committee room. Congressman Ray Thornton of Arkansas, Congresswoman Barbara Jordan of Texas, Congressman Charles B. Rangel of New York sat on the front benches; behind them sat Congressman Walter Flowers of Alabama and Congressman Jerome R. Waldie of California.

These members, and the others, in spite of their individual differences, despite their different backgrounds, despite their geographic diversity, despite their race, did actually represent an honest system of self-government.

When the time came to vote on Article I, the following members, among others, voted for the Article: Walter Flowers of Alabama, James R. Mann of South Carolina, Ray Thronton of Arkansas, M. Caldwell Butler of Virginia, Harold V. Froehlich of Wisconsin, all whites; and John Conyers of Michign, Charles B. Rangel of New York, and Barbara Jordan of Texas, all blacks.

At that point the past twenty-five years of American constitutional history seemed to fall into place. The House of Representatives, the representatives of we the people, were now representatives of all the people. Without regard to race they had deliberated on so important a question, and they had reached a decision worthy of constitutional self-government.

For the United States, the breaking of the caste system has been no easy triumph. During the 1960s assassinations took five of our leaders, but at last we have struggled up to the starting line.

We are possessed of new energy. In the eyes of the world we have earned new respect. Our purpose has not changed. We go forward resolved to prove what President Washington proclaimed after he took his first oath of office: "The preservation of the sacred fire of liberty and the destiny of the republican model of government," Washington said "are staked on the experiment intrusted to the hands of the American people."

Notes

1. United States v. Louisiana, 225 F. Supp. 353, 355 (E. D. La. 1963).
2. *Ibid.*, pp. 380-81.
3. United States v. Alabama, 192 F. Supp. 677 (M. D. Ala. 1961).
4. United States v. Wood, 295 F. 2d 772, 784-85 (1961).

5. James Howard Meredith, et al. v. Charles Dickson, Fair, et al., No. 19,475, U. S. Court of Appeals for the 5th Circuit, Sept. 28, 1962, New Orleans, p. 76.

6. *Ibid.*, p. 77.

7. *Ibid.*, pp. 78-79.

8. United States v. Mississippi, 229 F. Supp. 925, 974 at 974 (S. D. Miss. 1964).

9. United States v. City of Jackson, Miss., 318 F. 2d 1, 5 (5th C., 1963).

10. United States v. Mississippi, p. 998.

11. Burke Marshall, *Federalism and Civil Rights* (New York: Columbia University Press, 1964).

12. *Ibid.*, pp. 40-41.

13. Lyndon B. Johnson, "Special Message to the Congress: The American Promise" (March 15, 1965), *Public Papers of the Presidents: Lyndon B. Johnson, 1965* (Washington: Government Printing Office, 1966), I, 281-87.

14. U. S. Congress, House, Committee on the Judiciary, Subcommittee No. 5, *Hearings on Voting Rights*, 89th Cong., 1st sess., 1965, pp. 2-123.

15. Lyndon B. Johnson, "Remarks in the Capitol Rotunda at the Signing of the Voting Rights Act" (August 6, 1965) in *Public Papers*, 1965, II, 841-42.

16. South Carolina v. Katzenbach, 383 U. S. 301, 337 (1966).

17. United States v. Executive Committee of the Democratic Party of Dallas County, Alabama, 254 F. Supp. 537 (S. D. Ala. 1966) [Judge Daniel Holcombe Thomas].

18. *New York Herald Tribune*, December 6, 1965.

19. U. S. Congress, House, Committee on the Judiciary, *Hearings, Debate on Articles of Impeachment Pursuant to H. Res. 803*, 93d Cong., 2d sess., 1974, pp. 93-96.

20. *Ibid.*, pp. 110-13.

DONA BARON

7.

THE NATIONAL PURPOSE RECONSIDERED: A POST-BICENTENNIAL PERSPECTIVE

THE MOOD OF THE NATION at the time of the Bicentennial was more apparently one of cynicism and apathy than of sincere celebration. The advent of the Bicentennial Year opened the floodgates of over-commercialization and patriotic puffery. The culminating Fourth of July was a day for spectacle and, perhaps surprisingly, a genuine holiday spirit materialized and proved infectious. Yet, virtually no one—and certainly no national leader—seemed able to evoke the meaning of 1776 for 1976. In the era of Vietnam and Watergate few were to be found to speak seriously of a national purpose or to meditate upon how the nation might live up to it. Perhaps just as few were listening. The heroism of Bunker Hill, the sacrifice of Valley Forge, the thoughtful idealism of a Thomas Jefferson had given way to the vacuities and pious platitudes of the 1976 election campaigns.

Ignore it or not, however, the era of the Revolution *had* left a legacy, still intact, albeit showing the effects of stress and strain. That legacy to the people of the United States in 1976 was an explicitly articulated national purpose, a purpose forged during the Revolutionary era and spelled out in the Declaration of Independence and the Preamble to the Constitution. Our national purpose consists of a commitment to seek a set of lofty goals. Premised on belief in the value of respect for the essential dignity of the individual human being, our national aspirations relate primarily to liberty, equality, and justice. From this perspective the touchstone of government is the degree to which its activities do not impede but, if anything, facilitate and enhance each person's ability to realize his or her potentialities, to pursue happiness. The necessary corollary is government by consent of the governed which in the United States has taken the form of constitutional democracy. Thus the American national purpose should be understood as the pursuit of certain ideals which, by their very nature, can never be attained once and for all but must continually be related to the evolving processes and conditions of a dynamic society.

The Columbia University series of symposia, "The National Purpose Reconsidered: 1776–1976," was one of the few serious reappraisals conducted during the Bicentennial Year. Each of those who participated attempted to consider at least in part a basic question: How was the nation faring in relation to it fundamental values? The essayists focused upon broad aspects of the national purpose—equality and civil rights, constitutionalism, the relation between religion and the values of public life, America's role in global affairs, and America's economic health. The salient experiences of recent years—the Vietnam war, Watergate, the civil rights revolution, persistent "stagflation," and the energy crisis—provided the backdrop for these reflections upon America's enduring values. Taken as a whole this collection of essays is very much a creature of its time, manifesting the same tension apparent in the country at large in 1976, a tension between discouraging assessments of our prospects, on the one hand, and resurgent (if sometimes repressed) optimism on the other.

George W. Ball seeks to counter "the self-deprecation and self-flagellation that have characterized what might be called our post-Vietnam neurosis." Arguing that the United States by virtue of its history and "objective situation" must play a leading role on the world stage, he underscores the relevance of basic American values to foreign policy, and concludes affirmatively that "strong American leadership" is necessary to meet an admittedly formidable agenda of international problems.

Martin E. Marty comes to his analysis of recent trends in religion in America very much aware of the "anomie and apathy of the times." Although he explains how religion and religious commitments have become dissociated from civic life, Marty nevertheless concludes on a note of muted optimism. He projects the possibility that within local religious subcommunities selfish concerns will be overcome, and a new dialogue between religion and national purpose initiated.

Of the essays, Barry Commoner's induces the greatest pessimism. Perhaps this is because he considers so may intractable problems—the scarcity of resources, environmental degradation, unemployment, inflation, and dysfunctional bureaucracy, among others. According to Commoner, at the root of the popular malaise is the dissociation of social interests from operation of our economic system, and our apparent inabliity to confront this "basic fault." To solve this problem, Commoner suggests, we must determine how to establish institutional forms "consistent with the nation's unshakable devotion to political freedom" that will enable concern about major social goals to govern the functioning of the economic system. Yet, even after emphasizing the grave and fundamental nature of the dilemma, Commoner asserts that if we approach the issues with confidence we can discover "how to combine the economic democracy of socialism with a humanistic concern for personal freedom and a firm commitment to democratic government." In effect Commoner has argued that in order to surmount our crisis we must first of all be *optimistic*.

Affirming his belief that America "has not come to the end of its long march to become a more perfect union," Gunnar Myrdal observes that events of the past thirty-five years have confirmed his conviction that "in the longer run" the ideals comprising our national purpose "have determined the trend of development in America." Landmark Supreme Court decisions, the successful "Black Revolt" in the South and subsequent civil rights legislation demonstrated that the ideals of the national purpose could be activated as a social force crucially contributing to the shaping of public policy. Yet Myrdal makes clear that the nation's commitment to these basic ideals is far from unwavering. The pervasive social system of discrimination and segregation often called "racism" continues to prevent blacks from enjoying "real equality of opportunities." Social and economic reforms in the United States generally fail to extend down to the level of "underclass" of the poorest and most needy, a group disproportionately black. While it is difficult to achieve broad social reforms anywhere, Myrdal suggests that it is particularly difficult "in a country with such a peculiar reluctance to interfere with people's liberty to do what they please, and with so little homogeneity—racially, culturally, economically, and in all other respects."

John Doar, writing of changes in American constitutionalism, is the most positive. A participant in two of the great constitutional challenges of our time—the civil rights revolution and the Watergate impeachment proceedings—Doar's mood is one of celebration. While conceding that it will take many years "to correct the effects of the caste system," Doar unequivocally affirms the triumph of the civil rights movement in winning political rights for black Americans. By finally breathing life into the concept of citizenship expressed in the Fourteenth and Fifteenth Amendments, America has, in Doar's view, "at last struggled up to the starting line." Ultimately, Doar conveys confidence as he exhorts the American people to continue to demonstrate that to them "freedom, justice and equality" are not merely words.

This counterpoint of resurgent optimism, on the one hand, and cynicism, disillusionment and despair, on the other—so evident in the Columbia University Bicentennial symposia—provides a portrait of the United States of America upon reaching its two hundredth year and also facilitates assessment of the nation's prospects. After an era of trauma and at a time of difficulty, the grounds of despair were still sown with the seeds of optimism.

That there was in America such widespread doubt about the nation, its government, and its purpose can in no small part be traced to our adventures in Indochina.

For some Americans the shattering fact of Vietnam was that we lost. Their vision of America, fed by classic strands of American optimism and accomplishment and inflated by U. S. attainment of superpower status in the post–World War II era, was that America was different from other nations, not only more fortunate but somehow invulnerable. They could not accept that the war was lost in the deltas or the mountains but, rather, attributed defeat to some inadequacy of the political system or to a lack of moral fiber on the home front.

For others, America's basic purpose in the world of nations was made a cruel mockery by our intervention in Indochina. That fledgling confederation of 1776 which, on behalf of self–government and individual liberty, had fought against the greatest power of the time had two hundred years later become a superpower attempting to thwart a nationalist revolution by fighting on the side of an elitist, reactionary, an corrupt client state. The rhetoric of self–determination and freedom, stretched beyond the bounds of credibility, seemed to such critics a monstrous hypocrisy.

For many, fundamental American values were undermined by the methods used to fight the war. How could a nation whose sustaining principles exalted the dignity of the individual resort to the wanton destruction of B–52 carpet bombing or to the invasion of neutral Cambodia? What vision of justice could encompass a My Lai massacre? To those who asked came no adequate response.

Perhaps the most deleterious effect upon America of the war in Indochina was the damage done to the fabric of the American polity by the manner in which the government under successive administrations managed the war effort at home. The people of a body politic premised upon consent of the governed were led into war, and kept at war, by a government which attempted to gain and maintain support for U. S. involvement through the dissemination of increasingly transparent propaganda about the need for war and what came to be widely recognized as half-truths—and lies—concerning activities of both sides on the fields of battle and in the diplomatic corridors. The alleged ability of the President to command the best information and advice, as well as the supposed need for secrecy, were often used to deny the public information, to render impotent a Congress inclined to fecklessness, and to slur the patriotism of those in dissent.

The unhappy saga of Vietnam illustrated all too clearly how far American government had strayed from the model of 1787. Too willing to abdicate its responsibility for keeping government accountable, the public had been confounded and alienated by a miasmic "credibility gap." Government by consent of the governed had been travestied. There had arisen an "imperial Presidency" that would have appalled the Founding Fathers, a Presidency so arrogant that the thirty-seventh incumbent was to claim that where matters of "national security" are concerned the President is "sovereign."

The congeries of events subsumed under the heading of "Watergate" provided still another indication of how far the government *and* the people of America had departed from their purposes and values. Furthermore, Watergate constituted another blow to the national morale.

Watergate encompassed corruption of the Executive Power wedded to contempt for Congress and the people (the cover-up itself, the impoundments, the secret bombings of Cambodia, etc.); disrespect for the party system and the electoral politics of democracy (the burglary itself, the campaign "dirty tricks," the campaign contributions used to bribe or extorted for "protection," etc.); and infringements of civil liberties (the "enemies lists" and their use by the IRS, the Huston plan, the activities of the "plumbers," etc.).

One might argue that the unearthing of Watergate, the exposure of the President and his associates, the deposing of the President and the imprisonment of others involved in the scandal, the Supreme Court decision in the tapes case, and such remedial legislation as the Campaign Spending, War Powers, and Budget and

Impoundment laws represent not only a return of the system to what it should be but proof that the constitutional system really can function under tremendous pressure. After all, the press pursued the scandals; Congress ventilated the issues, deliberated and moved toward impeachment; the courts stood firm when it counted; the office of Special Prosecutor was created, persisted, and carried on the prosecution—and the public responded.

Yet, in all the relief and self-congratulation which followed the transfer of power on that day in August 1974, alarming symptoms of an infirm democracy were overlooked. Essentially, the contribution of "the press" was the work of a lone newspaper—the *Washington Post*. Its most vital revelations, which occurred during the electoral season of 1972, were virtually ignored by television and were mostly buried in the back pages of other newspapers. Meanwhile White House denials were given front page treatment. Congress did not exactly rush to investigate, nor were the activities of the Senate Select Committee on Campaign Practices unmarked by timidity. Although the House Judiciary Committee ultimately performed, as John Doar points out, in consonance with our finest constitutional traditions, for months its work was characterized by partisanship and seemingly haunted by a pervasive fear of regicide. While Special Prosecutors Archibald Cox and Leon Jaworski were resolute in pressing to gather evidence, Special Prosecutors Jaworski and Henry Ruth entered into a series of plea bargains resulting in greater punishment being accorded many of the "little fish" than most of the major perpetrators. Even as it rendered its great decision in *United States* v. *Nixon*, the Supreme Court, seeking unanimity, opened up new constitutionally legitimized loopholes for assertions of executive power and prerogative. That welcome honesty and candor which Gerald Ford brought to the Presidency was tainted by his full and complete pardon of Richard M. Nixon— an action which, while sparing further agony, stultified the still ongoing investigatory process and demonstrated how far we were from "equal justice under the law."

Nor did the public generally respond to Watergate in a manner equal to the hopes and ideals of the Founding Fathers. It was extremely slow to reach the point of outrage. Even then the public

was reluctant to follow the logic of the evidence, to conclude that
the President was guilty. By the time the American people generally came to think the President guilty, there remained widespread
reluctance to accept impeachment as the appropriate remedy. Just
as the public, finally, was prepared for impeachment, Nixon resigned—producing profound gratitude that it was all over and an
intense desire to repress memory of the dismaying events, rather
than to seek to learn what had gone wrong.

Much as we might applaud the steadfastness, courage, and
integrity of such men as Sirica, Cox, Ervin, Rodino, and Doar, the
events which transpired between June 17, 1972 and August 9, 1974
by no means conclusively demonstrated that "the system works."
We will never know if Mr. Nixon would have been forced from
office had he not installed the taping system or if, even after existence of the tapes was known, he had destroyed them. There is
much room for doubt.

Although Nixon carried the exercise of presidential power to
extremes, he was not the first imperial President. If the times seem
to require the strong leadership of an activist President, American
constitutionalism still mandates strict accountability. In recent decades, however, the American people and the elected representatives who reflect their wishes have proven to be more interested in
results than in methods and too willing to abdicate their responsibilities. It is this yearning for a benevolent despot in the White
House which provided the necessary context for the excesses of the
imperial Presidency and which casts a shadow across the prospects
of institutional reforms designed to invigorate the notion of presidential accountabliity and to limit the scope of presidential prerogative.

Both Gunnar Myrdal and John Doar write of recent advances
in civil rights. That progress, as each contends, indicates the vitality
of core values embodied in the national purpose. But, ironically,
the costs of this progress in terms of national self-confidence have
been great. Furthermore, social processes have been initiated
which involve at least as many feelings of frustration as of achievement.

So tortured were events of the 1960s that few took issue with

H. Rap Brown when he pronounced violence "as American as cherry pie." The fabric of the polity was badly ripped by the assassinations of the 1960s, which were often associated in the public mind with civil rights ferment. A few, looking for meaning in the murder of John F. Kennedy, attempted to suggest that, like Lincoln, he was a martyr for civil rights. To this day no one knows *why* President Kennedy was shot. What one does know is the damage his assassination did to the country. Almost all Americans felt immense grief, and a sense that the nation would never be quite the same. And then came the other assassinations—that of Robert F. Kennedy and of civil rights leaders Medgar Evers and Martin Luthur King, Jr. There were attempts on the lives of James Meredith, Governor George Wallace, and President Gerald Ford. Each further shook America's faith in its political processes, its government, and itself as a society. While each assassination took its toll, the ghetto riots of the 1960s further undercut America's self-confidence. In large part because the turmoil of the 1960s was so severe, by the time of the Bicentennial "We Shall Overcome" seemed more an anthem of nostalgia than of conviction.

Pride in recent strides in the area of civil rights is tarnished by realization of how late those accomplishments came, how near we yet remain to the "two societies," how much bigotry and how many residues of racism still linger. Furthermore, it may well be that what we have finally achieved are but the easy victories.

Increased emphasis on equality as a value has been reflected in court decisions, legislation, an reams of implementing regulations. But by now it has become apparent that busing is not the answer to intergrating the schools, let alone the society, and that school intergration *per se* is neither necessary nor sufficient to provide equality of educational opportunity. And while, as Gunnar Myrdal indicated, affirmative action programs have been relevant mostly to the least needy blacks, even broader questions remain unanswered concerning their constitutionality, efficacy, and wisdom.

In essence, American society is grappling with the most difficult aspects of the meaning of "equality": What is equality of opportunity? Can equality of opportunity produce other than equality of result? Is equality of result what we really should aim for? These questions are far more complicated than were the issues of *de jure* segregation of blacks; the ideals of the national purpose are now less instructive as guideposts for action. Furthermore, what "equality" and "justice" mean in America must be spelled out anew in a political environment far more complex than when the question seemed to be just the place of the black in the South. Now former allies in the civil rights movement of the 1960s sometimes find themselves pitted against each other. In many cases benefits accorded one group, or individual, result in quite tangible losses to another group, or individual. Now a bewildering variety of groups have learned the lessons of the civil rights movement and are seeking their own place in the sun. American society has been permeated by consciousness of group identification. Women, Chicanos, native Americans, homosexuals, the physically handicapped—and others—demand an end to perceived discrimination. Often they demand as well affirmative action or other forms of compensation to overcome the effects of past discrmination or indifference to their special problems.[1]

Even when there is progress—achieved without violence, by players observing the rules of the game—there may not be grounds for unmitigated elation. As Alexis de Tocqueville observed, "the desire of equality always becomes more insatiable in proportion as equality is more complete." Where there is greater equality, there is greater competition. If the barrier was once the privileges of the few, it soon takes the form of overwhelming numbers of "men . . . nearly alike." More fundamentally and disturbingly, Tocqueville concludes:

> Men will never establish any equality with which they can be contented. Whatever efforts a people may make, they will never succeed in reducing all the conditions of society to a perfect level; and even if they unhappily attained that absolute and complete equality of position, the inequality of minds would still remain, which, coming directly from the hand of God, will forever escape the laws of man. However democratic, then, the social state and the political constitution of a people may be, it is certain that every member of the community will always find out several points about him which overlook his own position; and we may foresee that his

looks will be doggedly fixed in that direction. When inequality of conditions is the common law of society, the most marked inequalities do not strike the eye; when everything is nearly on the same level, the slightest are marked enough to hurt it.

Such processes can cause a "strange melancholy" to haunt the citizens of democratic countries, even in the midst of abundance.[2]

Economic well-being has always been inextricably linked with the basic values comprising our national purpose. As Willard Hurst has observed, for two hundred years our society has held "that it will most likely achieve its goals if it works from a healthy material base; in other words, people are more likely to pursue the virtues of justice and equality if they are not driven by hunger or cold."[3] It was the economic chaos found under the Articles of Confederation that provided a strong impetus toward drafting the Constitution. The great debates between the merchant-oriented Hamilton and the agrarian Jefferson were not over the fundamental goal of assuring the well-being of all but over how to achieve it. When President Franklin D. Roosevelt pronounced "freedom from want" a part of "liberty" he was amplifying this basic value consensus for a now industrialized society.

The history of the United States has been a phenomenal story of successful economic development achieved by conquering a vast and rich land, overcoming obstacles to a national market, developing and mobilizing technology, and pragmatically abandoning nineteenth century laissez faire capitalism for the twentieth century semiregulated, semiwelfare state. Seemingly endless resources were exploited by a hard working and efficient people. Though wealth was not distributed evenly, no nation could boast having so large a proportion of its population enjoy the fruits of prosperity.

The 1960s saw the beginning of a new round of self-examination concerning the distribution of America's wealth. It was not difficult to compile an appalling roll of horrors: one-fifth of the population living in poverty (as federally defined); between six and twelve million suffering hunger and malnutrition; decay of the centers of the great cities, etc. A decade later, as Gunnar Myrdal observes, the "unconditional war against poverty" had lost its élan. The dilemma of poverty amidst affluence remained unresolved. A further cause for discouragement was the realization that whereas in the 1960s the basic economy had been expanding, in the 1970s it seemed to have lost its buoyancy.

Cyclical economic problems usually have had immediate, but relatively superficial and transient, adverse effect upon attitudes toward government and society. The economy has eventually rebounded and problems such as inflation and unemployment have been ameliorated. But the 1970s brought "stagflation"—a novel combination of unusually high inflation and greatly slowed economic growth with its concomitant, high unemployment—which continued to resist the cures applied. Thus the Bicentennial Year was seriously troubled by economic uncertainty and, worse, increasing pessimism about the nation's long-run economic prospects.

Socioeconomic problems which have already proven more lasting—the inequitable tax system, the welfare "mess" which satisfies neither the poor nor the rich, the dependence of major industries upon government action to perpetuate profits and power— have been even more corrosive in their effects upon the polity. Though they may still be considered remediable—theoretically unnecessary corollaries to America's generally impressive success in moving toward fulfillment of the national purpose in the economic sphere—their identification with vested interests and ineffective bureaucracies tends to discourage hope for solutions and to increase feelings of alienation.

Two great issues which have recently come to public consciousness raise grave doubts about the future of the nation and fundamental questions going to the core values of the national purpose. These issues can be labled "environment" and "energy."

Concern over the environment has resulted from realization that finally the frontier no longer exists; the land cannot be exploited without regard to consequences. Those who identify with the environmentalist cause often insist that our "throw-away economy" is bent and misshapen. While such jeremiads are widely accepted, they often serve to obscure the real dilemmas posed by the options. The environmental problem presents difficult choices—value choices. Environmental protection cannot come without costs in money, jobs economic dislocations, and the deferral, or sacrifice, of pursuit of other social goals. For example, while most would agree that air and water pollution are undesirable, and even that massive government expenditures to reduce them are necessary, it is less clear that in the long run the public will wish to pay the hidden costs—passed on in higher consumer prices by industry as their "share" of the "clean up." Although most would concur in the environmental soundness of the idea of recycling bottles, consensus comes less easily when it is found that the use of glass, rather than plastic, containers may cost thousand of jobs in the plastics industry. Thus it is with many of the current proposals. The quality of the environment cannot be preserved or improved without any trade-offs, and many of them will be painful.

If the environmental issue poses fundamental choices as to goals, the energy crisis offers none as to goals, only as to means. What is new is the growing perception of limits. If the environmental crisis teaches that more may *not* always be *better*, the energy crisis teaches that more may *not* always be *possible*. Technology may not always be able to come to the rescue. Technologically feasible solutions may not be economically feasible. The energy dilemma will force reconsideration of the allocation of both public and private capital resources. It also poses great questions about the efficacy of government and about civic virtue. Questions of competing sources of energy and of how—or whether—they should be developed are not within the purview of this essay. But questions about the ability of our institutions to cope with the energy crisis can be considered here.

Barry Commoner suggests that one structural flaw is at the root of all our economic problems—the failure of social concerns to govern effectively the functioning of the economic system. Rather than confront this central question, it is far more likely that our political system will continue to attempt the application of palliatives piecemeal. Neither our fragmented political structure nor our pragmatic political style is conducive to radical or comprehensively integrated therapies.

"Fragmented" is the single word which best characterizes the American political system. The constitutional system is one of federalism and, at the national level, "separated institutions sharing power." The congressional committee system, promoting specialization and the division of labor, further decentralizes decision-making processes. The bureaucracy of the federal government is a congeries of relatively independent power centers. All three branches of government interact with that vast array of interest groups which pullulate from our pluralistic society. The countervailing forces of integration must come from the political party system, presently in a state of decay. And, even at their strongest, American parties are more given to the aggregation of heterogeneous elements than to their unification. The other great force capable of encouraging integration is the office of the President— the activation of which risks resurgence of the imperial Presidency.

The American political style is pragmatic. Our usual approach to problems is instrumental rather than ideological. Our goals tend not to go beyond marginal or incremental improvement. Our *modus operandi* is bargaining and compromise. As a polity, America has almost always tinkered with problems.

The American political structure and style are mutually reinforcing. Historically, both have served us well. But will they suffice as we attempt to negotiate the "historic passage" into an era of constraints and limited resources? The possible scenario is grim: Congress, acting largely in response to especially potent lobbying groups, slices off pieces of a fairly comprehensive, integrated, presidential energy program. Some measures—mostly half-measures, not too well interrelated—are enacted. We attempt to muddle though. Valuable time is lost. Then comes the "crunch." Congress delegates to the President increased discretionary authority to impose stringent controls on manifold aspects of our economic life. Undoubtedly this responsibility and power will be conferred with little concern for the long run effects on constitutional democracy. American government will have continued its evolution into a kind of plebiscitory presidentialism.

We are facing not simply the question of how our institutions will respond to the problems of energy scarcity. The question is, more fundamentally, how will Americans respond? Can a society of self-indulgent individuals make the personal sacrifices necessary for *all* to maintain a reasonable standard of living? Successful negotiation of the "historic passage" will require nothing less than a reinterpretation of the meaning of individual freedom in relation to the commonweal.

The current "historic passage" will also clarify the nature of the nation's commitment to equality. Meaningful sacrifices will not be made unless there is the widespread conviction that what is demanded is demanded fairly, proportionately. It will be extremely difficult to convince most Americans that the basic operative principle is that, in the words of President Carter, "none of the people should be asked to bear an unfair burden, and none should reap an unfair advantage."[4]

Though the roots of our despair may run deep, the seeds of resurgent optimism may yet thrive.

If the wars in Indochina suggested obliviousness to essential American values, widespread domestic opposition nonetheless demonstrated the moral sensibility of millions. Despite incidents of repression, millions of citizens were able to protest their government's war—a remarkable sign of constitutional health.

There are, in addition, positive aspects of the Vietnam legacy. Through such measures as the War Power Act, Congress has attempted to restrain the imperial Presidency and to reinvigorate constitutional precepts of congressional responsibility and Executive accountability in the realm of foreign policy. The human rights initiatives of the Carter administration reflect a post-Vietnam repugnance toward playing the role of ally or of arms merchant to governments which would make George III's regime look enlightened. The moral backlash from Vietnam has led to closer public and official examination of other international activities, such as covert operations, which may be construed to be in the interest of external national security but which are not consonant with values basic to our national purpose. Most salutary of all, Vietnam may finally have brought a real recognition to Americans of America's limitations as an actor on the international scene. If we truly comprehend that we are not immune to the temptations of hubris or

the corruption which often accompanies the exercise of power, and
if we recognize that, as George Ball reminds us, external constraints must be seen to affect our objectives, then these under-
standings could provide the foundation for a foreign policy perhaps less ambitious or arrogant than those of the recent past, but
more consistent with *both* our professed values and what "realists"
call our national interests.

However slow American were to awaken to the implications
of both Vietnam and Watergate, we did nonetheless wake up—
and with a peculiarly American form of moral outrage. Most nations found the Watergate struggles bizarre and needless. But most
other cultures are more resigned than ours to the manifestations of
a flawed human nature. As Seymour Martin Lipset observed,
"Americans retain both the capacity to be shocked by evil and the
motivation to resist it."[5] If the nation's toleration of the accumula-
tion of power and of corruption in office is greater than two hun-
dered years ago, it still has its limits.

Watergate produced a spate of reform legislation: limiting the
possibilities for corruption in campaign financing, strengthening
the role of Congress in budget making, restricting the use of impoundment, repealing various measures which too readily allowed
creation of a "state of emergency" giving the President vast powers, and so on. Jimmy Carter's attempts to make the Presidency
more informal, low-key, accessible, and open represent another
reaction to Watergate. The "motivation to resist evil" also appears
to have produced internal reforms in the Internal Revenue Service,
the Federal Bureau of Investigation, and the Central Intelligence
Agency.

The fundamental question concerning the overall efficacy of
such reforms is one of will. As Benjamin Franklin said, our government is a republic—*if* we can keep it. The wisdom of a system of
"separated institutions sharing power" is compelling, as has so recently been demonstrated. But institutions and institutional reforms are not everything. If only time can tell whether we retain
sufficient "republican virtue" to overcome the countervailing force
of the desire to "escape from freedom," the fact that Watergate

and Vietnam have engendered reforms and heightened sensibilities suggests that republican virtue is far from dead in America.

In no aspect of our recent history can greater cause for optimism be found than in the area of civil rights. Given that for three centuries the treatment of blacks in Amerrica ran directly counter to the values of the national purpose, it is indeed remarkable how much was achieved in a single generation. Recent American advances in this realm are all the more astounding when it is appreciated just how intractable the problems of racial, ethnic, tribal, and religious differences have proven in other lands—whether the regime be democratic, authoritarian, or communist. Just look at Northern Ireland, Cyprus, Burundi, or the Soviet Union—to name but a very few!

Furthermore, what has been accomplished in the area of civil rights in America has been accomplished within the framework of the constitutional system, even if tactics sometimes pushed at the borders of that system. The civil rights revolution came about through the exercise of First Amendment rights and through litigation. Courageous, energetic men, some of America's best, such as Martin Luther King, Jr., Thurgood Marshall, Earl Warren, and John Doar, worked within the political system they still respected to rectify age-old injustices. Blacks led the way. The Supreme Court contributed firm leadership. The Executive Branch and Congress caught up. Within a generation the Jim Crow apartheid of the Old South had been broken. Black Americans at last had been effectively integrated into the political system: South and North. Discrimination in public accommodations became but a faint memory. Real progress had been made against job discrimination. And, despite all the mutterings of "white backlash," the sensibility of most Americans to the degradation that is racism had been increased—irreversibly.

The social revolution was not, however, just for and by blacks. Indeed, the past fifteen years have witnessed a social ferment and expansion of rights comparable to the Jacksonian and New Deal eras. The changes wrought by the women's movement clearly will be immense. And while it may yet be premature to judge, one can at least be sanguine regarding the benefits Chicanos, native Americans, homosexuals, and the handicapped will gain from raised consciousnesses and new laws. Still other categories of the sociallly marginal—criminal defendents, prisoners, the mentally ill, juveniles, aliens, and illegitimates—though less active as organized interest groups, have been the beneficiaries of a judicial expansion of rights. The extent to which these judicial decisions will amount to more than changes in "black letter law," again, cannot be answered at this time. What can be asserted, with both pride and hope, is that America—largely because of the way the values of the national purpose serve to channel and inform social processes—is virtually unable permanently to define outgroups.

The past twenty years have witnessed a promising recasting of American constitutionalism. *Federal* judicial power had been invoked to guarantee citizens basic rights *within* the states. If the inability to rely upon state courts and state governments to adhere to constitutional norms affecting the blacks was the prime cause of these developments, momentum has nevertheless carried the reinvigoration of basic values of the national purpose into other realms. Federal courts, especially the Supreme Court of the United States, read fundamental constitutional clauses through new spectacles, developing a new jurisprudence of equal protection, due process, freedom of expression, and personal privacy and autonomy. Congress, too, has vastly expanded the rights of American citizens with the enactment of such laws as the Civil Rights Act of 1964, the Freedom of Information Act, and the National Environmental Protection Act. Concurrently, both Congress and the judiciary have developed novel techniques for scrutiny of the activities of executive officials and regulatory commissions. Interestingly, with the slowing of these trends by the Burger Supreme Court, state supreme courts have begun to read their own state constitutions so as to expand for their own residents the breadth of protection from arbitrary governmental activity.

Ironically, the energy crisis may in the long run prove to have been a blessing in disguise. The current administration is attempting to present the impending energy shortage as a crucial challenge to the American people—"the greatest challenge that our country will face during our lifetime."[6] To meet this challenge citizens are exhorted to demonstrate understanding, maturity, courage, vision, imagination, ingenuity, and a sense of common purpose. Fortunately, since the costs of failure would be great, this is the kind of challenge the American people just might be able to meet. Appeals to higher instincts are not necessarily doomed to failure, as has been demonstrated many times in our history. As a people, we have manifested a bent for both technological and social inventiveness. Our recent social history suggests an interest among sizable number of citizens in achieving a leaner lifestyle—more in balance with nature and less oriented toward material acquisition as a value in itself. The energy shortage could very well serve as a catalyst, releasing new bursts of resourcefulness and renewing dedication to the values of the national purpose. Successful confrontation of the energy shortage, furthermore, would significantly bolster the nation's self-confidence.

As we enter our third century there are, then, grounds for a resurgence of optimism. The optimism which pervades each of the essays on the national purpose is not without legitimate bases.

Furthermore, it is significant that the then obscure former governor of Georgia was able to strike a responsive chord when he went to the electorate with an appeal to their latent optimism and self-confidence:

> I want . . . to have our nation once again with a government as good and honest and decent and truthful and fair and competent and idealistic and compassionate, and as filled with love, as are the American people.[7]

The persistence of optimism, despite Vietnam, Watergate, the wrenching 1960s, and the current tangle of socioeconomic problems, may in fact be a crucial determinant of the nation's future. Optimism can be a self-fulfilling prophecy. Moreover, various characteristics of the partially submerged American optimism can continue to vitalize the values of the national purpose.

Though its precise effects are difficult to pin down, optimism, belief that one's own efforts can shape the future and anticipation of the most favorable results—in other words, hopeful activism—is a key sociological variable. In countries where, instead, fatalism, resignation, and pessimism prevail—Argentina, for example—one usually finds a complex of social, economic, and political problems more dire than those of the United States. Hope has tended to spring eternal in the American breast, and that hope tended to justify itself.

The essays written for Columbia's "The National Purpose Reconsidered: 1776-1976"—whether or not one fully accepts their analyses or prescriptions—both demonstrate and inspire confidence. Attentive to history, the essayists are more interested in learning from it lessons applicable to the present than in tormenting themselves with perceived failures. They stress the relation of ideas to practical problems. They see reality as complex and do not scorn an incremental approach to solutions. In essence, what these men are saying is that at the time of its Bicentennial America was beset by serious problems. Since these problems would not go away by themselves, they would have to be fully confronted. The results of grappling with these problems might prove to look more like amelioration than conquest—but "let's get on with it!"

When these men urge us to try to meet the challenges of striving toward the ideals with which the United States has been— and should remain—identified, it is difficult to resist. That public figures as thoughtful as these are not abandoning the struggle should augur well for the future.

The cynicism, disillusionment, apathy, and despair so widely perceived during the Bicentennial Year may have been more apparent or superficial than real. Certainly there were clear signs that America was a healthier and more hopeful nation than might have been expected after the years we had just been through.

Notes

1. This paragraph was, in part, inspired by the unpublished comments of Professor Charles V. Hamilton made following Gunnar Myrdal's address, "Race and Class in a Wefare State," at Columbia University, October 2, 1976.

2. Alex de Tocqueville, *Democracy in America*, Phillips Bradley, ed., Henry Reeve, trans.; as revised by Francis Bowen (New York: Vintage Books, 1945), II, 146–47.

3. Willard Hurst, "Consensus and Conflict in Twentieth-Century Public Policy," *Daedalus; Journal of the American Academy of Arts and Sciences*, "American Civilization: New Perspectives" (Fall 1976), p. 93.

4. Statement of President Jimmy Carter, dated April 29, 1977, in Executive Office of the President, Energy Policy and Planning *The National Energy Plan* (Washington, D. C.: Government Printing Office, 1977), p. iii.

5. Seymour Martin Lipset, "The Paradox of American Politics," *The Public Interest*, "The American Commonwealth—1976," no. 41 (Fall 1975), p. 153.

6. President Jimmy Carter, "The Energy Problem," televised address to the nation, April 18, 1977, in U. S. Office of the Federal Register, National Archives and Record Service, General Services Administration, *Weekly Compilation of Presidential Documents* (April 25, 1977), 13(17):560.

7. Jimmy Carter quoted in Phil Stanford, *Jimmy Carter*, Capitol Hill News Service, Citizen's Guide to the 1976 Presidential Candidates (Washington, D. C., 1976), p. 31.